LOVED FEARLESS

Rachael Sanowski

Clarkdale House

Requests for information should be addressed to:
Clarkdale House, LLC, 2075 Clarkdale St., Detroit, MI 48209

The names and details of many of the individuals depicted here have been changed to protect anonymity.

Cover design: Rachael Sanowski
Cover photo: Christoph Sanowski
Chapter Title photos: Rachael Sanowski

First Printing: February 2018

Printed in the United States of America

ISBN-978-1-5323-6717-5

DEDICATED TO THE MEMORY OF MY NANA, HELGA WILLIFORD,
WHO WAS NEVER IN A HURRY TO BE ANYWHERE ELSE WHEN I WAS WITH HER.

Contents

Acknowledgments

I want to thank Stefanie Norlin for editing my rough draft with a writer's eye and a disciple's heart.

Thanks to Paul Propson, more like a pastor than boss to me, for making space at Covenant Community Care for dreamers and their dreams.

Thank you, Van Den Bosch Gospel Foundation, for helping me realize a relational health retreat and curriculum and growing my courage to write a book.

Thank you, Lily Group, Loved Fearless retreat participants, and praying women of Charlotte Mason Community School for entering the wide-open spaces with me.

Finally, I am eternally grateful to my family and friends and Father in heaven, who know me best and still love me.

Prologue

This book is about relationships, and it is meant to be read in relationships.

I've tried to be honest and alive in these pages, but the only way I can share past moments of relational wrestle and shimmer is to capture them in words. And then they are no longer free. They are in a relationship zoo.

I have to keep living relationship beyond these pages.

And I want you to live relationship as you read these pages.

I like to read autobiographies, but I would much rather be hearing the stories live and living out new chapters with the tellers. I like listening to recorded worship, but I would much rather be in a room with worshipers listening to the Spirit and each other for the next note and the next word and the next song together!

In the same way, I know that if you will make some space with a few other people to not only read this book but also be open books to each other, God will do more in and through you than you could ask or imagine! Afterwards, you'll exclaim, "The book wasn't bad, but being together was AMAZING!" There is nothing new under the sun, except what happens between us and an infinite God when we risk knowing and loving each other.

Introduction

How I wish...

The wall between us is so thin
Just a cry would break it in
And I, I think I heard You
Wish for a friend who is not sleeping
Somebody who would wait in the garden
Somebody, how I wish it could be me[1]

Before he died, Jesus had a beautiful dinner with his closest friends. He washed their feet. He spoke from his heart. He encouraged them to be good friends who listen to each other and know each other and lay it down for each other. He told them he was going to his Father but that his Spirit was coming to live in them for good. He prayed for them, that they would really know him and love him. His friends listened and said, "We see you. We know who you are. We believe you came from God."

Jesus said, "The hour is coming when you will all scatter, each to his own home, and leave me alone."

And they did. That night.

After supper, they went out together into the moonlight, crossed the Kidron Brook and entered the Garden of Gethsemane. Jesus was heavy-hearted. His friends were heavy-lidded. He prayed and wept. They slept. Then Judas showed up, with priests and armed soldiers. Jesus said, "I AM the One you want. Let the others go." And they went. Each to his own home. John made it into the high priest's palace, where Jesus was being questioned. Peter hung around in the courtyard for a while, but then *he* was being questioned: "You're Jesus' friend, right? Your accent gives you away. Didn't I see you with him in the garden?"

"No, No, NO!" Crow... crow...[2]

---

1 Becker, Margaret. "Cave It In." *Falling Forward.* Sparrow Records, 2008, CD
2 From the Gospel of John, chapters 13-18

It *could* be me

Jesus entered the garden of Gethsemane, and to follow him means to daily walk into the garden of decision and surrender—*God's will or mine?*—on my way to the garden of paradise.

I have heard Jesus wish for a friend who would be with him in the garden. And I *do* wish it could be me. Just like the rich young ruler wished he could have eternal life. And all his stuff, too. I don't want to choose between this life and the next. I want Jesus, but when it comes to pain and death, like Peter on the peripheral of decision, I'd rather sleep than cry. I'd rather lie than die. *I don't know this Jesus you're talking about, for Christ's sake. Leave me alone and let me warm myself by the fire.*

David said to God, "Because your steadfast love is better than life, my lips will praise you."[3] I wish I could have God's love *and* my life, because I like doing things my own way. As a kid, I listened to Billy Joel on vinyl:

> I don't need you to worry for me cause I'm alright
> I don't want you to tell me it's time to come home
> I don't care what you say anymore, this is my life
> Go ahead with your own life and leave me alone[4]

I am learning that preserving my life, in the sense of proving myself right and getting my own way, is a sure way to be left alone. And loneliness is a slow and painful dying. If I am avoiding the garden to avoid pain and death, it's not working. It takes violence against others to get my own way, to not listen, to not care, to not come home. It takes violence against my own heart to shut it down and not let anyone into it. Keeping hurt out means keeping love out, too, which hurts a lot.

I see that I cannot love God *and* do my own thing any more than the rich ruler could love God and hold on to all his stuff, because one desire is motivated by love and the other by fear. Love and fear don't mix. And they don't tie. When one wins, the other loses. When Peter let Jesus wash his feet, love won. When Jesus' friends really believed that he was from God, love won. When Judas left the meal to make good on his silver and tip off the arresting party, fear won. When Peter denied knowing Jesus, fear won.

---

3 Psalm 63:3
4 Joel, Billy. "My Life". 52nd *Street*. Columbia Records, 1978, LP.

The good news is, when Jesus surrendered to his Father's will, love won. When he forgave those who crucified him, love won. When he rose again, love won. Jesus has made a way for love to win in our lives every time we choose love over fear.

Choosing love

When I first listened to *Love is a Choice*[5] on audio cassette in college, it woke me up to my true thoughts and feelings about myself. I realized that I did not believe I was loved. I believed I could work at being admired, but not loved. I also believed that who I was deep down was not admirable, so I needed to keep people from discovering the real me. I avoided doing things I was awkward at and put my efforts into what came easy. My words and actions were motivated by a need for love and a fear of being discovered unlovable. The heaviness of this is the absolute futility of it, like wishing to be in the garden while refusing to enter. The truth—that I did not believe—was that people could have (probably would have) loved me if I had given them the chance to really know me. However, my endless performing and showing off intimidated people and discouraged relationship, because it felt like a competition (and we were only competing in my best events). The *Love is a Choice* tapes made me aware of my co-dependence. There are a lot of definitions out there, but I understand co-dependence as a fear-based relationship. When love didn't seem like an option, I looked for relief from the fear of rejection by pursuing relationships that I tried to control but couldn't, which compounded my fears, instead of relieving them.

For me, feeling unlovable is like struggling to breathe without an external source. Co-dependence is finding that source in a person. It's not that I believe the person loves me or that I even love the other person. But I have come to believe that I need that person around, at any cost, in order for me to breathe. My motivation in the relationship is fear of dying without it, even if the relationship is killing me.

The concept of love being a choice used to frighten and anger me, because I believed that love had not chosen me. But the beauty of the garden is that Jesus chose me (and you) over his own life. He died to live with us forever. Love has already won, and nothing can change that.

Entering the garden is believing this is true.

---

5 Hemfelt, Robert, et al. Love is a Choice: Recovery for Codependent Relationships. Thomas Nelson Publishers, 1989.

Harlem

What happens to a dream deferred?

Does it dry up
like a raisin in the sun?
Or fester like a sore–
And then run?
Does it stink like rotten meat?
Or crust and sugar over–
like a syrupy sweet?

Maybe it just sags
like a heavy load.

Or does it explode?

Langston Hughes, 1951

Exploding Dreams

Ivy-covered stone house remnants, midtown Detroit 2008

Being human is a dream deferred

Langston Hughes' poem about Harlem[6] makes me think about being human. God created us in his image and set eternity in our hearts. In the first garden, Adam and Eve were beautiful and knew it. They were living in paradise. They were walking and talking with God. They were whole, until they listened to the serpent instead of God, and it contaminated their very being. They tried to hide the shame by hiding their bodies, but the ugliness was coming from the inside out.

And *their* internal ugliness has become *our* ugliness.

We have inside us the shame of what we are not and the longing for what we were meant to be. We were made to be perfect, and we are not. We were made to live forever, and we are dying. So, we work at cultivating beautiful things outside of ourselves, hoping that a good appearance will hide, maybe even *transform*, the sin-ravaged ruins of our hearts. Some of us try to have relationships outside of ourselves. We try to be admired without being known. Or we admire others without knowing them and try to make them a paradise to dwell in, away from the ugliness in our hearts.

Jesus' friend, Peter, struggled with this. He had dreams of greatness and freedom from tyranny, and he recognized Jesus as the Messiah who would make his dreams come true. Jesus said, *YES! I AM! I will suffer and die to make your dreams come true!* Peter resisted: How is suffering leadership? How is death victory? This shall never happen. And Jesus responded: *It has to happen. Only Satan will get his dream if it doesn't.*

Surrender is the way into paradise. This is not the death of a dream. This is the *explosion* of a dream.

Jesus loved Peter. He was entrusting him with the keys of the eternal kingdom. He wanted to be with Peter forever. But his Father was requiring that Jesus die for Peter's sins in order that they could have a relationship that would never end.

Not long after this conversation, Jesus took Peter and the Zebedee brothers up to a mountain and gave them a glimpse of what happens when a dream explodes and the dust settles. Death gave way to life, as Jesus changed into *Himself* before their eyes. His face shone like the sun, and his clothes went white as light. Moses and Elijah appeared, like witnesses and keepers of the dream. Peter wanted to set up camp on

6 Langston Hughes. "Harlem". *Montage of a Dream Deferred*. Holt, 1951

this mountain of dreams coming true, until a bright cloud appeared and a voice from the cloud said, "This is my Son, the Beloved, with whom I am well pleased; listen to him." Peter, James and John fell on their faces, full of fear. Jesus came over to them and touched them. His words to his friends were: "Rise, and have no fear."

This is death and resurrection. This is a dream deferred exploding into a better dream.

Peter wanted to protect Jesus and keep him close. He wanted heaven on earth, where his loves would be safe and with him always. But heaven on earth is a dream deferred by sin. In relationships, we have to let the dream of heaven on earth explode and make room for a better dream. Although this will look differently in each relationship, a key to love detonating fear is trusting the Father. When Peter said, "Far be it from you, Lord, to suffer and die," he was asking Jesus to choose what he wanted over his Father's will. And Jesus replied, "Get behind me, Satan!"[7] Jesus trusted his Father's will over Peter's will. This is love. Love always trusts. People shift, our hearts condemn us, but God never changes. And he has good gifts for us.[8] So, when we love God by listening to him, we are making room for a better dream than fear could ever realize. While Peter was focused on his fear of losing Jesus, Jesus was focused on how love of the Father could overcome that fear and keep them together forever.[9] When Peter drew his sword in defense of Jesus, Jesus said,

> Put your sword back into its place. For all who take the sword will perish by the sword. Do you think that I cannot appeal to my Father, and he will at once send me more than twelve legions of angels? But how then should the Scriptures be fulfilled, that it must be so?[10]

While Peter was focused on protecting Jesus from physical violence, Jesus believed that his Father could rescue him at any moment, so he stayed focused on his Father's will to end *spiritual* violence through obedience onto death.[11]

What happens to a dream deferred? We can choose what happens to it. Sometimes, like Peter, we are so afraid of losing a dream that we become violent in our arguments and efforts to save it. But despite our best efforts, it continues to fester and weigh us down. We can choose instead to bring our rotting dream to God and experience the quiet revolution of love detonating fear and remaking us from the inside out.

---

7 From the Gospel of Matthew, chapters 16-17
8 Malachi 3:6; James 1:17
9 John 3:14-15
10 Matthew 26:52-52
11 Philippians 2:8-11

The heart of God

The only paradise on earth that can be ours is the heart of God. As we let go of self-preservation and follow Jesus into the garden of surrender (*Not my will but yours, God*), we find God and live. The way to transfiguration is exposing our hearts to the light of his love. The way to greatness is a shrinking and emptying. When we die to the dream of a good performance bringing us closer to paradise, we make room for a better dream: I already am. It has already been done. God loves me, and nothing can separate me from his love.[12]

God's heart is found in Jesus' words and actions. Jesus is the Word that is with God and *is* God. He was homeless and stripped down in order to make his home in *us* and be our treasure. His single ambition was to mirror the Father's heart and give away everything for love.

> He who did not spare his own Son but gave him up for us all,
> how will he not also with him graciously give us all things?[13]

God's heart is full and generous, and there is no fear in it. He knows us and loves us. He gives us what we cannot give him. He trusts us to *trust* him. Trust is the only thing we have to give him. Trust is the only way into his heart. To get there takes exposure and fear exploding in and around us. I think of Peter, so ecstatic and privileged to be in the presence of a victorious Jesus and a few close friends. It fed a dream of belonging to a beautiful place with beautiful people. Peter wanted to stay there and make it his reality, to the exclusion of all other realities, even the reality of his own heart. When a bright cloud overshadowed them and the radiant awareness of God shed light onto Peter's heart, he was terrified at the exposure. *The One who truly has the power to free me or kill me is looking right at me. What will He choose? What is my fate?*

"Rise, and have no fear."[14]

When we listen and believe at the point of total disclosure, religion explodes into relationship, and we are free to love and be loved without constraint. Transfigured by God's heart that is toward us and in us, we are no longer afraid of God leaving us or not liking us but are instead completely surrendered to the power of his love transfiguring us all.

---

12 Romans 8:35-37
13 Romans 8:32
14 Matthew 17:7, John 3:16-20

After the miracles on the mountain, Jesus and his friends came down to a crowd of people and a suffering boy in need of healing. But his friends couldn't heal the boy. Jesus was angry with them[15] because they didn't trust him. Trust is the beginning of relationship and reciprocity. They had stopped believing in the relationship and were relapsing into religion.

I was reading this passage with friends one Friday evening, and some were struggling with Jesus' reaction. Why was he so sweet and tender on the mountain when his friends were afraid and then so angry at them when they didn't have enough faith to cast the demon out of the boy? One woman said, "I don't want Jesus to be mad at me. What Jesus am I going to get when I come to him, the tender one or the mad one?" She was wondering if Jesus was safe. I am wondering if Jesus was just responding in love to his unsafe friends. He was spending all his time with them, showing him who he was and telling them who they were, and they still didn't believe. I see him loving them by sharing his frustrations with them, trusting that they would listen and act on what they heard.

When a relationship is young, there's euphoria and politeness and a fear of stepping on the other's toes. As love grows, so does courage to be known and confess sins and disappointments. When Jesus shares his frustrations with us, it's a privilege. It's deeper love. It means he trusts us to love him more, as we know him more. Trust is an ongoing conversation. Just like Jesus and his friends talked out their stuff, we have to keep talking out our stuff with him and *listening* to him, like the Father instructed from the cloud. This is how we stay close to God's heart.

Passion without trust

Almost six hundred years before Jesus was on earth, the exiled Ezekiel got a supernatural glimpse at some dreams in need of exploding. He was in his house in Babylon with some other exiled Jewish leaders when the Lord's hand fell upon him and a fiery, shimmery human form took Ezekiel by his hair and spiritually teleported him "between earth and heaven." Ezekiel sees the temple in Jerusalem and an idol in front of the north gate entrance, where an altar used to be. Then God takes him to the door of the inner court, where there's a hole in the wall. The inner court was a holy place, for the priests and the Levites to be in the presence of God, but now it's a hole in the wall, open to the carousing public. Ezekiel digs through the wall and reports:

15 Matthew 17:17-20

> There, engraved on the wall all around, was every form of creeping things and loathsome beasts, and all the idols of the house of Israel. And before them stood seventy men of the elders of the house of Israel, with Jaazaniah the son of Shaphan standing among them. Each had his censer in his hand, and the smoke of the cloud of incense went up. Then he said to me, "Son of man, have you seen what the elders of the house of Israel are doing in the dark, each in his room of pictures? For they say, 'The LORD does not see us, the LORD has forsaken the land.'"[16]

This is a post-Eden, pre-Jesus time in the world, when the only access to the heart of God was in the temple, where the glory of God rested above the Ark in the Holy of Holies. The only people allowed to physically enter this holy space were the Levitical priests. They entered on behalf of the people and offered animal sacrifices as atonement for the people's sins. But then it shifted. The people gave wanted his ways but their own ways, too. They wanted his love but did not want to love him exclusively. They replaced the altar of repentance with an idol and sacrificed their connection to the holy heart of God. In the absence of God's loving presence, their fears and emptiness grew. They went to the temple, but God's glory was not there. Maybe they thought it was because God was not trustworthy and had abandoned them, so they were on their own to find relief and self-fulfillment and a god that would satisfy. Their search led them to whoring after whomever and whatever and looking at dirty pictures in the dark. And that was before the Internet.

I don't know how these religious leaders wandered so far from the heart of God, but I know how it happens to me. I sin or am sinned against (for the millionth time), and I don't want to deal with it. I don't want to confess or forgive anymore, so I just stay away from my heart and God's and look for distraction away from him. Eventually, what I turn to for relief takes me prisoner, and I figure I deserve my sentence, so why even ask God to bail me out? After a while, I am mad at him, too, because he has left me alone, like he left the temple, once the Jewish priests had desecrated it.

Love is a choice, and God lets us choose whether we will love him or not.

---

16 Ezekiel 8:10-12

An ongoing conversation

Whatever it is that has its hooks in you, you will never be free from it until you find something you want more. It's not about getting rid of desire. It's about giving ourselves to bigger and better and more powerful desires.[17]

I can't think of a more powerful desire than to be known and loved by the *first and the last, and the living one* who holds the keys to Death and Hades.[18] But fear gets in the way of this desire: fear that the Lord does not see us or want us. To believe that he knows us and loves us takes an ongoing conversation.

Five hundred and some years after Ezekiel, Jesus came to be the one sacrifice that could make it right again between us and God. So, when Jesus' closest friends didn't believe that love could drive out demons, heal epilepsy and *raise the dead*, it grieved him. But he didn't give up trusting them to get it eventually, and he hasn't given up on us either. Before he went back to heaven, he assured his friends that it was better for him to go, because then they could have his Spirit living inside them. Their hearts could be the new temple where the Spirit of God lives and communes.

God *loves* us.

Much of our *doing* is rooted in the fear that this may not be true. God has given us his Spirit to remind us that it *is* true.[19]

Fear-based *doing* does not re-establish a lasting paradise on earth. It just clutters the temple of our hearts with selfish ambitions and idols. Love-inspired *being* gives the Spirit permission to explode our fearful flesh dreams and make room for the dream of God's love setting up paradise in our hearts.

How does this work? How do we talk to each other? The apostle Paul said to pray in the Spirit at all times.[20] What does that *mean*? How can I do *one thing* all the time, especially something as mysterious as praying in the Spirit, when there are so many other things to do?

---

17 Bell, Rob. *Sex God: Exploring The Endless Connections Between Sexuality And Spirituality*. Zondervan, 2007.
18 Revelation 1:17-18
19 John 16: 7-11
20 Ephesians 6:18

Pause is the real Play

Be still and know that I am God.[21]

I have a friend who used to be afraid to be still.

Our kids went to school together. We spent an hour together each week, praying for the kids and staff at the school. It started with praying verses over the children and teachers. It grew into worshiping and opening our hearts to God before interceding. I started catching glimpses of Kate's heart, and I liked what I saw. I told her I would like to take her to lunch some time. She laughed and said that a friend had wanted to take her for a birthday lunch a few months earlier, and it still hadn't happened.

Several months later, we had lunch together. The food was delicious, and the time together was sweet. She went home wondering why I wanted to hang out with her.

We kept worshiping and praying Wednesday mornings. Sometimes, it was like having breakfast with the Spirit and wondering why he wanted to hang out with us. We entered the sanctuary (the school met in a church) like overworked cooks, keeping the Spirit at a distance, praying for our children because it needed to be done. But like Jesus gave Martha permission to leave her worries and dishes and come close, the Spirit kept giving us permission to want and be wanted. To *be* and not do. To enter the sanctuary of our hearts, where he was growing a garden.

One cold December Wednesday, six of us gathered around the Baby Grand and started singing:

I just want to breathe. Teach me how to lean. I labor now to rest. Show me how to love...[22]

Take my heart, I lay it down at the feet of you whose crowned.
Take my life, I'm letting go. I lift it up to you who's throned.

It's just You and me here now...[23]

Songs are just words and notes, and we are just flesh and bones, until the Spirit inhabits the praises and his people. The Spirit inhabited us that morning. As we

21 Psalm 46:10
22 Misty Edwards (live from the prayer room)
23 David Crowder Band. "Only You". Crowder, David, et al. *Illuminate.* Sixsteps,

prayed, I got really warm and my heart started beating quickly. I started praying that the Word would sink deep into the soil of our children's hearts...that we and our children would let God be our shield, rock, King, fortress, water and warrior. God gave up his *Son* to be these things for us. I was weeping. My hands were raised. The other women were weeping and praying with me. We had lost ourselves in the garden of his presence.

Later that day, I got a voicemail from Kate: "I just wanted to let you know...I love seeing God with you. Thank you for the refreshing moments this morning. For making space and being real. And being with me in it, too." The Spirit of God was changing us, from the inside out.

Kate had been running the children's ministry at her church for years. She was really good at it. And she was tired. She wanted a break. From doing. For a while. She took a month off from church work. She started reading Song of Solomon and Henri Nouwen. She frequented the RiverWalk and let the river breezes and the fresh wind of the Spirit refresh her body and soul. When the month was over, she wasn't ready to go back to the busyness. So, she took another month off. To *be* for a while.

> Awake, O north wind, and come O south wind! Blow upon my garden, let its spices flow.[24]

> I am my beloved's and my beloved is mine. He grazes among the lilies.[25]

I met her at the RiverWalk one morning at the end of her second month of rest. She was anxious about re-entry. She had so enjoyed the pause in the busyness. She was not excited about pushing *play* again. So, I asked her: Who says *that* was the life you are supposed to live and *this* is not? Who says that way of *doing* instead of this way of *being* is the Kingdom way? What if this *pause* is the real *play*?

I asked if I could pray for her, and she said, yes. I held onto her hand, closed my eyes, felt the sun on my face. I wanted to pray but could not speak. I felt the heaviness and glory of the Spirit's presence silencing me. Kate started to cry. She must have felt it, too. Finally, I said, "Holy Spirit, keep saying what you are saying to us. I have nothing better to say." It was beautiful and hidden. Like a garden growing in our hearts.

It started us on a journey of being still and testing the hypothesis that pause is the

24 Song of Solomon 4:16
25 Song of Solomon 6:3

real play and the Spirit really wants to hang out with us. We invited other women into it and called it the Lily Group. This was the invitation:

Desire.
There is resistance to being desired.
By God.
To desiring God.
To the two desires becoming one.
But God's desire for us is real.
The joy that motivated Jesus to endure the cross
was desire for us,
His church bride.
And our desire,
dampened by disappointment,
staved off by ambition and addiction,
is for our Bridegroom Jesus.
The Lily Group is a space for believing
that as we,
fragile and beautiful like lilies,
open ourselves to desiring and being desired,
the Spirit of God
will browse among us
and awaken us to love.

In the wide-open space of *pause,* the Spirit spoke. We listened and responded, and pretty soon we were having the conversation. He led us to our clutter and helped us make more room for him and the garden he was growing in us. When we left that space, the space in our hearts for him was still wide and accessible in the rhythms and responsibilities of the day. And just as we had been still and present to his coming near, the Spirit, too, was open and desiring for us to return and browse and remember love.

Gold in Clay Houses

> We have this treasure in jars of clay, to show that the surpassing power belongs to God and not to us.[26]

When Jesus was on earth, he had to hope in and hold on to things he could not see. On his wilderness fast, he had no external assurance of God's love and trust-worthiness. But he believed in it, regardless of appearance or circumstance, and it defined who he was. After weathering the elements without food or friends for forty days, he was hungry. The tempter came with an offer to alleviate his hunger in exchange for bread, care, and power but at the price of Jesus' soul. Instead of forfeiting the paradise within for some temporary relief, Jesus entered it and found nourishment and defense against the lies.[27]

When on trial before Pilate, Jesus faced a similar temptation. He was on trial for saying he was God, and the Jewish leaders wanted him crucified. He had been beaten and mocked and forced to wear a thorn crown. When Pilate asked him where he was from, Jesus did not answer. Pilate asked, "You will not speak to me? Do you not know that I have authority to release you and authority to crucify you?"

Jesus' enemies were ripping into his flesh and his psyche. He was standing there with nothing but the paradise within. Jesus answered him, "You would have no authority over me at all unless it had been given to you from above."[28] In other words, *God's got me. You can kill me, but you cannot have me.* This is the treasure that will not die. This is the *internal* paradise that gets us to the *eternal* paradise. Many nights before Gethsemane, Jesus was meeting his Father in gardens and mountains and wherever he could get alone with him. He was cultivating a love dream, an eternal connection. He was finding the heart of God and letting it grow in his heart. Death cannot kill this.

> I have been crucified with Christ. It is no longer I who live, but Christ who lives in me. And the life I now live in the flesh I live by faith in the Son of God, who loved me and gave himself up for me.[29]

Our flesh is a clay house, mud like and fragile. And all that we clothe and surround ourselves with is, in essence, just as breakable. But not the treasure within.

---

26 2 Corinthians 4:7
27 Matthew 4:1-11
28 John 19:10-11
29 Galatians 5:1

The Lily Group was about making space for this treasure. At the first meeting, there were seven of us. We read from Song of Solomon 1:4. "Draw me after you; let us run. The king has brought me into his chambers." We took time to be alone with these Words. I felt like the Spirit was asking me, "What do you really want to tell me?"

I'm scared.
I want to feel safe but I don't.
What if...I can't let you...nurse me to health?
What if...I can't receive what you want to give me?
This is withdrawal.
I'm letting go of thinking that you just want me to perform well
and just want me to help *others* heal.
I'm walking towards the belief that you *want me.*
To be with you.
To heal and be done with fear.

My performance dreams were cracking and bulging. I was trying to keep them in, and the pressure was intense. I was shaky and exhausted after the first group. My body was tense with fear, and I did not feel able to talk myself down from it. I was afraid of not being enough for God and those women. I was afraid of being exposed and found wanting. But I had entered. The garden. His chambers. The space of desire. The Spirit was going to help me settle down. He was telling me that I did not have to *do* anything to be free. He was going to meet me in my fear and desperation. *He* was going to free me.

We all had different reactions to that first Lily Group. Sam felt the Spirit come upon her like a massage, only better. Liz said she felt when we were worshiping and praying that if she didn't praise him, she would burst. One woman shared from her heart with tears. And never came back to the group. And I was panicking inside.

Why was being still and knowing he was God terrifying me? I know now that I had put so much of me into a twisted way of following but not really following him. I tried to be god to others or make others god in my life more than I let God be God. To acknowledge this was painful and explosive. But the truth was also freedom and provision: freedom to be human and provision so others could be human. It felt crazy to admit that most of my energies went into rescuing and being rescued. I would have to let go of addiction, identity, my own wisdom and capacity. It wasn't much, but it was all I had. I mean, who wants to be stripped down to clay? Letting go was the price of entering the garden with the treasure hidden in it.

Dreaming God's dreams

We come into this world tainted with knowledge and sin. It is not safe or beautiful. God is not with us, at least not automatically. We only gain His presence through believing again. It's when we believe in him that we become new creatures. Our belief makes us children of God again, children of eternity.

> If anyone is in Christ (s)he is a new creation. The old has passed away; behold, the new has come.[30]

Beauty restored. Our task restored. *Simplified.* The yoke of keeping the law exchanged for the yoke of his love and enoughness. We don't have to be our own gods or find our own gods anymore. We don't have to fend for ourselves or make a name for ourselves anymore. We just have to believe, and by *believing* we have *life* in his name.[31]

That is God's dream for us.

It is easier to describe dreams connected to performance and achievement than to describe God's love dream revolutionizing our hearts. A little girl who dreams of playing professional soccer immerses herself from a young age in the practice of soccer. Her diligence at working hard at the necessary skills, combined with her natural ability, determine whether or not her dream comes true. A young man who dreams of becoming a doctor dedicates himself to a prescribed course of study over a set length of time. His academic and applied performance determines whether or not his dream comes true. If I have a dream of growing bananas in the Bahamas, I have to *do* something about it: acquire some capital, move to the Bahamas, and cultivate a banana plantation, at the very least. But when it comes to God's dream for our hearts coming true, it is often the *doing* that gets in the way.

The second Lily Group was about saying goodbye to the performance dreams that needed to explode to make room for something better. We read some more from Song of Solomon 1:

> My mother's sons were angry with me; they made me keeper of the vineyards, but my own vineyard I have not kept! Tell me, you whom my soul loves, where you pasture your flock, where you make it lie

30 2 Corinthians 5:17
31 John 20:30

down at noon; for why should I be like one who veils herself beside the flocks of your companions?[32]

When we had time to be alone with these words, I settled into a big red chair and listened to Misty Edwards in my headphones. I had my Bible and journal close, but it felt like work to open them. It was hard enough to just take deep breaths. I let my head and neck sink into the side of the chair. I tried to lean my heart against God's heart, like Misty was singing. Once I had listened through, I plugged it into the speaker for all of us. At the first group, I had led worship from the keyboard, but that had been fear-inducing for me. I needed to labor to get free of fear. I heard Kate beginning to cry next to me, and I reached for her over the big chair arm. I could just reach her arm with my fingertips.

When we broke the silence to share what we heard and confess our goodbyes, Liz said she was realizing that she has needs, and she wants to say goodbye to pushing those needs down. I shared that I wanted to say goodbye to my fear of women and my feelings of inadequacy as a woman. Shay said she wanted to say goodbye to not trusting God and his answers to her questions. Kate said she wanted to say goodbye to making sure others were ok and not being ok herself.

We prayed for each other and dreamed God's dreams for each other. Shay was crying for me. And I started crying, too. She saw me fighting for freedom and safe places for women and dreamed that I, too, would experience freedom and safety. The women took turns loving me with their prayers, and I let them. At one point, I was thinking, this is too much attention on me. We should pray for someone else now. But I let it go. They were detonating my performance dreams and drawing me into the garden of God's abundant love.

A few days later, as I was listening to worship music and writing, my head started to feel heavy and my neck started to relax. I felt like I should lay down and close my eyes, so I did. I felt so peaceful lying there. I could feel the muscles in my neck relaxing in little tingly pulses. I remembered how the Spirit said I didn't have to do anything to get free from my fear. And so, I just lay there, enjoying the Spirit's presence erasing the tension from my neck and back. The joy was so encompassing that I laughed out loud. This was my *goodbye* to doing and my *hello* to holy surrender.

---

32 Song of Solomon 1:6-7

Enemies

Guardhouse, Historic Fort Wayne, Detroit 2003

Catching Foxes

> For we do not wrestle against flesh and blood, but against the rulers, against the authorities, against the cosmic powers over this present darkness, against the spiritual forces of evil in the heavenly places.[33]

> Catch the foxes for us, the little foxes that spoil the vineyards,
> For our vineyards are in blossom.[34]

Because of Jesus, our hearts can be a garden. He is the seed that enters to grow there. As we surrender to his love and our need for it, beautiful things start to grow in us, and others are attracted to the beauty. However, there is constant attack on the fruits of his Spirit growing in us. Temptations come like foxes, seeking to spoil our thoughts and actions. In the garden, we awaken to spiritual realities: God is strong and loving;[35] the devil deceives and destroys.[36] Whenever we get caught up in fighting God or self or others, the spiritual forces of evil (our real enemies) defeat us.

One Monday, not long after the supernatural massage, a situation triggered fear and disappointment that spiraled me into feelings of rejection. I saw in my mind one of those Scooby Doo Haunted House walls that turns if you move the right book and swings you around into a secret room. I was in the secret room of self-loathing. I cried out to God, feeling like a fake, like someone barely holding on to her sanity. I sat down at the piano and started playing and singing, "Come into my garden." I thought of a woman my husband and I prayed for who said there was an animal inside her stomach that we roused with our prayers. *There is a self-destructive animal in me, too.* I thought of the lover, saying to his beloved:

> A garden locked is my sister, my bride, a spring locked, a fountain sealed. Your shoots are an orchard of pomegranates with all choicest fruits...with all choice spices—a garden fountain, a well of living water, and flowing streams from Lebanon.[37]

I asked God, "Why would you say that? You know the neglected state of my garden. Then it came to me: God is a dreamer! He always trusts and always hopes. That

---

33 Ephesians 6:12
34 Song of Solomon 2:15
35 Psalm 62:11-12
36 John 10:10
37 Song of Solomon 4:12-15

settled me some, but the foxes were not so easily disbanded.

At lunch time, Kate came over. We ate lunch, then had coffee by the wood-burning stove. "Are you going to talk to me?" she asked. She knew I had been tumbling. I told her about the secret room and the self-hate that was keeping me away from love. It felt like love was planted in shallow soil, but there was something deeper, something toxic that was choking it out. Kate said, "I'm looking at you, and I love you." I knew it was true. And I knew the secret room was a reality, too. "I'm not afraid of that room," she said.

I warned her that I didn't even know what was in there. We started praying. My friend's prayers came in sobs. I was taking deep breaths, but not peaceful ones. My insides were shuddering with each exhale. I started to pray, and deep sobs came out of me. I do not remember the words, only that I wanted to be free. At some point, my legs, hands and neck started tingling, like needles were poking me. And then my hands locked up. I could not move them. They were burning hot.

We were in the secret room, and we were not alone.

Kate was sitting next to me, with one hand on my arm, one hand on my head. I was squirming around, like I was struggling to get free. I kept kicking my legs. Kate was interceding for me with words and tears. She kept telling me not to fear and that we were going to win. It was getting late. I felt this pressure to snap out of it, go back to business as usual, get my kids from school and make dinner. But my hands were crippled up and rooted to my sides, and I was numb and tingly in lots of places. Kate called her husband, and he offered to pick up their boys. "I am not going to leave you here," she said. I told her I was sorry. "DON'T say you're sorry" she said. "I am full of such peace, Rachael." I could tell that she was. The room was full of it. She dug back in. At some point, she felt tingling and burning in her hands, too. And this startled her. She thought, *Not me, too. Not now.* "I am going to stand for you," she said. She stood behind me, praying. I was saying stuff as it came. My legs and neck stopped tingling, but my hands and my heart still burned. I cried out to Jesus and proclaimed him as victor. I confessed my fear, my pride, my self-hate. I was desperate for him to have me completely.

> I am sorry for not giving you your joy. I want to give you your joy. I want to be IN Christ. I want consummation. I want the ecstasy of union with you. I want to lose myself in you. I need your blood to cover me, cleanse my mind, my lips, my heart. Place ME as a seal upon your heart. Write MY name on your hands. You died for ME. Your blood was shed

> for ME. Jesus, Jesus, Jesus. I don't know what I am fighting. I don't want to be fighting YOU. So, I am going to just surrender to you and let you fight for me.

Kate was cheering me on, saying, "We win! We win. He is fighting for you, Rachael." My hands were still crippled up and burning, but I saw a finish line.

> He is delighting in you, Rachael. He so delights in you. No wonder there is such a battle. No wonder Satan is holding on. Because you are a lover. And you won't stop fighting. You will keep bringing others to freedom. You will keep dreaming. Oh, he is delighting in you.

Then, she burst into pure, beautiful laughter. "He loves your sense of humor. He wants to share his humor with you." I wish I could have seen what she was seeing, but she was seeing it for me. She was infusing courage and faith and joy into me. She started singing, "His banner over you, his banner over me, his banner over us is love, love, love."

After an hour or so, I stopped squirming. It felt like I was done fighting. My hands were still crippled up and burning, but I was coming to rest. We were quiet for a while. "What next, Holy Spirit?" I asked. I told Kate she could sit next to me and still *stand*. She took my stiff and only half feeling hands into hers. "It's a tightness around my wrists, like at my pulse," I said. She felt the tightness. "When you said you weren't afraid of the secret room, I bet you didn't know THIS was in there."

She said, "I didn't tell you all of the dream."

"What dream?" I asked. "The bird dream?" She nodded. Six months earlier, Kate had a dream where we were worshiping together with others, and a birdlike thing flew into the room, but it was actually a demon. And it started oppressing us. It grew bigger and bigger, and all Kate could say was *Jesus, Jesus, Jesus*. And right before the thing almost consumed us, it disintegrated and disappeared.

"In the dream," she said, "I was standing over you, praying for you. I thought, that can't be right. Rachael would be praying over *me*."

"Who's the dreamer?" I asked.

"Maybe we both are," she smiled.

The next morning was worship and prayer at the school. I started playing, *There's Something About That Name*,[38] and it was filling me up. I was so excited. So thankful. I felt joy like helium. I couldn't stop smiling. Kate was standing behind me, so I couldn't see her, but I could imagine her trying to keep herself from lifting off the ground. The songs were victory songs, and I felt like I was bursting with victory. The secret room wasn't secret any more. It was wide open, and Jesus was in there in Spirit, filling it with radiant light. After we sang, *you are the glory and the lifter of my head*, I asked Kate if we could sing more words from Psalm 3 over the teachers. She smiled and said yes. We dug in. Resting, worshiping, warring. We prayed for the teachers and our children and our husbands, that God would be their glory and the lifter of their heads.

These things happened to me after I dared to enter the garden. Dying to self-sufficiency and coming alive to the love and power of God can unleash a variety of supernatural craziness. When Jesus died, the temple curtain ripped, the earth shook and went dark in the middle of the day, and dead people came out of their graves. When he rose, angels appeared, he walked through walls, caused hearts to burn, and breathed his Spirit into his friends. And as his friends came alive to his love and power in them, the opposition that had followed Jesus became *their* opposition.

A garden locked up is non-threatening and uninteresting. A garden alive is exhilarating and inviting to good growth and weeds, seekers and thieves. The key to extracting the badness and protecting the goodness is staying exposed to love. The difficult part about this, at least for me, is that I don't want to be exposed when I feel darkness and madness seeping into my psyche. I want to hide till the clouds pass. But hiding from love when I need it most exposes me to more fear. In an effort to protect myself, I am neglecting and not protecting the garden. Dying to self-sufficiency means letting God and others in. When our hearts and minds are faltering, we need the Spirit more than ever. And we need other dreamers to remind us of God's dreams for us, when weeds block our vision and foxes steal our courage.

Talking to God with an open heart is not necessarily clean like a Hail Mary. I used to find prayer a lot less wild when my heart was locked up. And a lot less thrilling. It takes trust to stay open to our hearts and his. It takes trust to invite others into an untamed growing relational space. If I had known that afternoon that praying with Kate was going to expose and paralyze me in her presence, I might have opted out. But the Spirit had prepared her for this with the dream six months earlier. And also by taking her the week before into a deeper surrender and spiritual freedom than anything she had previously experienced. All of this is assurance to me that the God who loves us has gone before us and will go ahead of us to let love win in our hearts.

---

[38] Gaither, William J. & Gloria. "There's something about that name." *Bill Gaither Trio*. CMG, 1970, LP

Offensive Jesus

I had an English professor and mentor in college who taught me about love, hate, injustice, creativity, hope, courage, collaboration and social engagement. He has profoundly influenced the way I think and live, and I admire him greatly. The one place we could not go together, though, was to God. He told me he was an atheist. When I asked why, he said it was because he could not believe in a God who was just sitting on his hands while so many people in the world are suffering.

I have spoken to many people who keep their distance from God for similar reasons. They do not trust God, because they are not certain whether he is an enemy or a friend. Because where *is* God when really bad things happen? If he is strong and loving, why doesn't he *do* something about all the pain and suffering and injustice?

These questions make me think of John the Baptist, sitting in a prison dungeon in the palace of Herod Antipas. John had relinquished all other ambitions and became a wilderness prophet, preparing the way for the Lord. He drew crowds, stirred hearts, baptized the ones who believed. When some religious people came to the Jordan where he was baptizing, John called them vipers and warned them to really turn to God or be cut down. When he saw Jesus, though, he said, "Behold, the Lamb of God, who takes away the sins of the world."[39] He believed Jesus was the real deal. He was staking his life on it. And then, after all of the sacrifice and testifying about Jesus, he was thrown into prison for commenting on Herod's personal affairs.[40] In that dark and lonely place, John seemed to need assurance of who Jesus was and what he was about. He sent friends of his to find Jesus and ask him, "Are you the One who is to come, or shall we look for another?"

> Jesus replied, "Go and tell John what you hear and see: the blind receive their sight and the lame walk, lepers are cleansed and the deaf hear, and the dead are raised up, and the poor have good news preached to them. Blessed is the one who is not offended by me.[41]

I see in Jesus' answer the way of the garden. Jesus was not sitting on his hands while John was in prison. His focus was on the garden paradise to come and on his love and power growing a garden in people's hearts. He assured John that he was doing what he was sent here to do. He encouraged John to not be offended by what he was doing and not doing. He commended John in front of the crowd for his greatness. But he did not try to get John out of prison, and John never got out. He was killed there, in

39 John 1:29
40 Mark 6:17-18
41 John 11:3-6

part because of Herod. Not long after, Jesus was killed, in part because of Herod. In this, too, John prepared the way for Jesus. But death is not the final outcome for either of them. In the end, love wins. And Herod loses.

Jesus was about healing people's bodies and speaking truth to their hearts. He came to start an eternal relationship with those who want him and believe in him.

> For God so loved the world, that he gave his only Son, that whoever believes in him should not perish but have eternal life. For God did not send his Son into the world to condemn the world, but in order that the world might be saved through him. Whoever believes in him is not condemned, but whoever does not believe is condemned already, because he has not believed in the name of the only Son of God. And this is the judgment: the light has come into the world, and people loved the darkness rather than the light because their works were evil.[42]

Love is a choice, and Jesus chooses to love. To demand love in return is not love anymore. Love lets the other choose. God lets us choose to believe him or not; to love him or not. When we choose love, his Spirit lives in us and transforms us from the inside out. But that does not necessarily transform the world around us or extinguish the suffering we experience. We live in a world cluttered by the consequences of unbelief and unlove. There are times when we will be victimized by those consequences and possibly offended by a Jesus who does not seem to be doing anything about them. The best thing we can do is come to him when we're offended, like John the Baptist did (through his friends). And his Spirit will reassure us, that he *has* done something and *is* doing something and *will* do something about it, that may not prevent physical harm or even death but will bring eternal life to our souls.

Exposure to love

Sometimes the fiercest battles are internal. Situations can trigger emotions and responses that bring on feelings of shame and an impulse to retreat. Disappointment in relationships, for example, can trigger shame and rejection. At least it does for me. When I am anticipating time with someone I care about and it does not happen when or how I expect it to, I sink into disappointment. Then shame creeps into my head and heart and taunts me for caring so much and reacting so intensely. Finally, I retreat into fear that I am not fit for relationship and am better off alone. Because I

42 John 3:16-19

do not want to expose myself or anyone else to more pain, I disconnect from God and the people who love me. Although exposure to love would bring freedom from shame, I disconnect from love and get blistered by shame and bombarded by lies.

When I am convinced that *I* am the enemy that should be sequestered and punished, I give the *real* enemy permission to tear me up from the inside out. If the enemy sabotages my garden with bad seeds and I feed them and let them grow, they can strangle the love and forgiveness and trust growing in my garden. Or if shame is a fox that I give permission to prowl in my head and heart, it will. And it will destroy the goodness growing there.

People handle disappointment differently. A friend told me that his disappointment *blocks.* When he feels emotionally threatened, he throws it back on the other person; he finds fault with the other person instead of himself to avoid letting the disappointment get under his emotional skin. So, his disappointment does not trigger *shame*, but rather *anger*, and if he does not come to God and the other person with that anger, different kinds of weeds begin to grow: "People are stupid and cannot be trusted. I am better off alone. I don't need them anyway. I don't need anybody." He turns away from love and relationship and begins seeing *other people* as enemies. In either case, the real problem is doubting that God—or his children—can be trusted.

Remember what Jesus did when He was alone and faced with temptation?

Instead of forfeiting the paradise within for some temporary relief, Jesus entered the internal garden and found nourishment and defense against the lies. In both examples above, it is a relapse into *unbelief* that endangers the garden. The way back to health and safety is exposure to love by finding the heart of God again.

> For we do not have a high priest who is unable to sympathize with our weaknesses, but one who in every respect has been tempted as we are, yet without sin. Let us then with confidence draw near to the throne of grace, that we may receive mercy and find grace to help in time of need.[43]

I think of Jesus saying, "Repent for the kingdom of heaven is at hand,"[44] and, "The kingdom of God is in the midst of you."[45] Jesus is the detonator of performance dreams. He is not saying, *Do better*! He is saying, *Come near. I am right here. The kingdom grows wherever we are in relationship*. The new dream is a relationship dream.

---

43 Hebrews 4:15-16
44 Matthew 3:2
45 Luke 17:21

So, we fight enemies, real and imagined, by re-entering the relationship. It will not help to pull at weeds and yell at foxes without returning to the heart of God. I feel shame for being *weak.* I feel shame for letting another person have the power to disappoint me. The legitimate cause for shame, though, is that I stop believing that God—or anyone—would want me near if I am so *weak.* Repenting in this case is turning away from performance or fear-based thinking and turning toward love, even in doubt, like John the Baptist did. When disappointed and unsure, I have to expose myself to love, so that love can cover me with the knowledge that God is for me, and I am his.

Bread, care, and power

If I keep my distance from God and other people because I have decided that they are against me, and I keep my distance from my own thoughts and feelings, because they trigger inadequacy and shame, who's left to hang out with? What's left to fill my mind and heart with? That's when shame and unbelief throw open the doors to the spiritual forces of evil. The devil comes close and tempts us to *virtually* live and *vicariously* love, so we can avoid the pain of relationship.

When the devil tempted Jesus in the wilderness, his strategy was to get Jesus to disconnect from his Father as his love and life source. He tried three different approaches, and each approach focused on meeting a legitimate need through power moves instead of through healthy relationship.

The devil first tempted Jesus to turn stones into bread. Jesus was hungry, and he had access to stone-mutating power. However, to do so would supersede a healthy relationship with food. Food has to *grow.* There is a God-created process to it. Jesus' hunger was real, but his hunger did not rule him. He was ruled by the words of God. God spoke the world and its order into being:

> "Let the earth sprout vegetation, plants yielding seed, and fruit trees bearing fruit in which is their seed, each according to its kind, on the earth."[46]

And it was so.

God made man and woman in His image. He made them out of one flesh, to stay one flesh. He blessed them and said to them:

---

46 Genesis 1:11

> Behold I have given you every plant yielding seed that is on the face of all the earth, and every tree with seed in its fruit. You shall have them for food.[47]

He did not give them stones to eat. He gave them food in abundance that would keep reproducing, and man had the privilege of living in healthy relationship with God and his creation. In contrast, the devil's temptation, then and now, is to satisfy hunger at the expense of relationship. I love how Jesus brings everything right back to relationship. He knows what we need to fill our bodies and souls and wants to give it to us:

> Ask, and it will be given to you; seek, and you will find; knock and it will be opened to you.[48]

Asking, seeking and knocking are essential to living in relationship.

> Which one of you, if his son asks him for bread, will give him a stone? Or if he asks for a fish, will give him a serpent? If you then, who are evil, know how to give good gifts to your children, how much more will your Father who is in heaven give good things to those who ask Him![49]

We cannot be fed well outside of healthy relationship.

Next, the devil tempts Jesus to throw himself off the temple and let angels catch him. Maybe to prove that he was God and that the Scriptures about angels applied to him.[50] Jesus said to him, "Again it is written, 'You shall not put the Lord your God to the test.'"[51]

Jesus *was* God, and it's wrong to test God. But more than just a test of deity, this temptation is a challenge to be known and cared for. The devil wants him to do something spectacular to force angels to act on his behalf. However, to create a need so that someone else will feel compelled to meet it is manipulation. This is trying to feed a hunger outside of healthy relationship. I know a little boy who likes to practice being a soccer goalie. Sometimes, when his mom shoots a sweet goal that he cannot block, he fakes an injury. He feels bad about not blocking the shot, so he tries to get his mommy to care for his non-existent injury instead of bragging about her skills. It

47 Genesis 1:29
48 Matthew 7:7
49 Matthew 7:9-11
50 Psalm 91:11-12
51 Matthew 4:7

may seem like a subtle difference between accidentally falling off the top of the temple and *throwing* oneself down or suffering an injury and *faking* one, but it is the difference between love and fear, truth and lie. A healthy relationship is based on love and truth, and there is nothing truthful or loving about manipulating people into paying attention and caring. Jesus pays attention to our legitimate needs and wants us to receive care in healthy relationship with him and others.

We cannot be cared for well outside of healthy relationship.

For his third temptation, the devil promises Jesus the world, if he will just bow down and worship him. Then Jesus said to him, "Be gone, Satan! For it is written, "'You shall worship the Lord your God and him only shall you serve.' Then the devil left him, and behold, angels came and were ministering to him."[52]

The trade is power for worship. We can sell our souls to capitalism, popular opinion, technology, sex, another person, the devil, but these transactions will not increase our power or value in the long run. We are owned by what we worship. Jesus takes the devil's temptation and flips it on its head:

> If anyone would come after me, let him deny himself and take up his cross and follow me. For whoever would save his life will lose it, but whoever loses his life for my sake will find it. For what will it profit a man if he gains the whole world and forfeits his soul? Or what shall a man give in return for his soul?[53]

We have no eternal power or value outside of a healthy relationship with God. When we choose the garden way of surrender, he restores our souls and shares everything he is and has with us.

The defeated enemy

We are in a battle against the dark spiritual powers that make their moves through people. People seem like enemies when they are listening to enemies and acting like enemies. But the real enemies, the devil and all the demons under him, were defeated by the love and power of God. Jesus loved and obeyed God to the death. Then God raised him from the dead, defeating the power of sin and death. Jesus said to his friend, John, in a vision: "Fear not, I am the first and the last, and the living

52 Matthew 4:10-11
53 Matthew 16:24-26

one. I died, and behold I am alive forevermore, and I have the keys of Death and Hades."[54] So, too, when we live in the garden of surrender, God's power and love come alive in us. We defeat the real enemy with God's power, and we diffuse the enemy's influence over people with God's love.

Here are some ways Jesus did it...

Once, after crossing the sea of Galilee, Jesus met a wild-looking man who lived among tombs and didn't wear clothes. He sometimes cut himself with rocks. People had tried to subdue him by force, but he would break the chains with his bare hands. The man had demons living inside of him. When Jesus met him, he did not try to subdue the man by force. He did not avoid him. He did not try to make friends with him. He commanded the demons to come out of the man. And they came out.

> Then people went out to see what had happened, and they came to Jesus and found the man from whom the demons had gone, sitting at the feet of Jesus, clothed and in his right mind, and they were afraid.[55]

The rescued man wanted to stay right there, at the feet of Jesus. He begged Jesus to let him stay close. But Jesus told him to go back to his home and tell the story of God's triumph over the enemy in his life. The wild-looking man was never the enemy, but he had enemies within that needed to be defeated in order for love to win in his life.

Another time, Jesus, tired and thirsty, was resting by a well, when a Samaritan woman came to draw water. The woman did not know Jesus, and yet she had reason to believe that he was an enemy, not because of what she saw in him, but rather because of his affiliations. The Samaritan woman said to him, "How is it that you, a *Jew*, ask for a drink from me, a *woman* of *Samaria*?"[56]

Jesus had never met the woman, but he knew her. He knew her deeper than race and gender and religion. He knew her history and her heart. He knew her thirst. She was not an enemy. The real enemy was false worship. Jesus said to her,

> "The hour is coming, and is now here, when the true worshipers will worship the Father in spirit and truth, for the Father is seeking such people to worship him."[57]

---

54 Revelation 1:17-18
55 Luke 8:38
56 John 4: 9
57 John 4:23

The Father is seeking men and women of all races to worship him, just as he is—holy, impartial, spirit—together, truthfully, just as they are—broken and thirsty. Jesus wanted this for the Samaritan woman, and he had to disregard the enemy's attempts at putting up barriers of *otherness* between the quenching of his thirst and hers.

A final example is when Peter told Jesus that He would never suffer and die and be raised the third day:

> [Jesus] turned and said to Peter, "Get behind me, Satan! You are a hindrance to me. For you are not setting your mind on the things of God, but on the things of man."[58]

Peter was Jesus' friend, but he was speaking like an enemy. He was speaking like Satan, who promised to give Jesus everything, if he would just forsake the words and ways of God. Jesus knew he was on earth to draw people back into the garden of eternal relationship with God, and he knew the only way to do it was to defeat the power of the enemy by entering the garden of Gethsemane and being killed on a cross.

> "Now is the judgment of this world; now will the ruler of this world be cast out. And I, when I am lifted up from the earth, will draw all people to myself."[59]

Peter was saying, it doesn't have to be this way. When the devil tried this in the wilderness, Jesus said, "Be gone, Satan!" But when Peter tried it, Jesus said, "Get behind me, Satan!" Peter was speaking like an enemy, but he was not the enemy.

Jesus did not send Peter away; he told Peter to get behind him. Instead of leading Jesus into temptation, Peter needed to *follow* him and submit to him, as to God.

These are three of many examples where Jesus faced the defeated enemy and put him back in his place of defeat, not by physical force but by spiritual force. Because Jesus followed God's words and ways to the death, Satan ultimately lost the war. However, he can win a lot of battles in our lives through fear tactics, if we let him. When we die to unbelief and we surrender to God's words and ways, his Spirit starts growing a garden of power, love and self-control in us.[60] That does not mean that fear

58 Matthew 16:23
59 John 12:31-32
60 2 Timothy 1:7

automatically leaves us, but it is defeated. It is like the enemy himself. Jesus refers to Satan as a strong man but to himself as the stronger man.

> When a strong man, fully armed, guards his own palace, his goods are safe; but when one stronger than he attacks him and overcomes him, he takes away his armor in which he trusted and divides his spoil.[61]

We were Satan's palace, and our sins were his goods. But Jesus attacked and bound the strong man when he died for us and our sins. If we let this be true, if we let Jesus' death be our death and his life be our life, we take away Satan's power in our lives. Many of us try to camouflage our fear and shame of being found out as sinners with a good front and an impressive performance. But all of our sins have been exposed and paid for on the cross. Jesus' perfect love can drive out all of our fears, and we can take back from Satan all that belongs to Jesus, by the power of his name.[62] Satan is the defeated enemy—not just in our hearts and minds but everywhere and in everyone. If we come across a wild-looking, self-destructive person, we do not have to fearfully write him or her off as a dangerous freak. We can face the inside demon and tell it to go, because his master is defeated. If we come across someone we have been told is not like us, we do not have to fear the otherness or vilify the other, because Jesus is our peace and our water. We are all equally thirsty and in need of a resting place of pure worship. If friends start talking like enemies, we do not have to fear that they are right and we have to listen, or, conversely, that they are so wrong we have to send them away. We can just put them behind us and keep following the words and ways of God. And if fear tries to get us in a chokehold, we can expose it to God and a trusted few and then command it to GO, in Jesus name!

What does love look like?

> You have heard that it was said, 'You shall love your neighbor and hate your enemy.' But I say to you, love your enemies and pray for those who persecute you, so that you may be sons of your father who is in heaven...If you love those who love you, what reward do you have?[63]

Jesus is talking about *human* enemies here, not Satan, the defeated spiritual enemy. When it comes to humans, neighbor or enemy, love is the protocol. So, the question is not, who's my neighbor and who's my enemy, but rather, what does love look like?

---

61 Luke 11:21-22
62 I John 4:18; Matthew 12:29
63 Matthew 5:43-46

After a parent criticized and belittled her daughter in my presence, I asked her, "Do you love your daughter?" She said, "Of course I love my daughter. She means the world to me." Not long after that, I was talking to God about the ease of showing compassion to a stranger in my office but not to my husband. And the Spirit whispered: "Love keeps no record of wrongs. Do you *love* your husband?"

Love is not a constant or a state of being (unless you're God). Love *chooses* to be patient, kind, content, humble, gracious; it chooses not to insist on its own way, to not be irritable or irritating; to keep no record of wrongs; to bear, believe, hope and endure.[64] When I do not choose these, I am not loving. We say *I love you* to people close to us, but what does that mean? Maybe it's like voicing a commitment to choose love. But it is not the choice itself. Love is an action. And another. And another. When I choose to not be kind to my husband or friend or child, I am behaving like an enemy. When someone who says she loves me is rude or impatient or resentful towards me, she is behaving like an enemy, which is frustrating, but doesn't need to be devastating. Although she is not choosing to love me in that moment, my response is still to love her: turn the other cheek, go another mile, strip myself of defenses. And pray. Because there is a battle underway. But it is not against flesh and blood. I should not resist the one who does evil, but I should resist evil, and evil will flee.[65] I should resist the temptation to defend, offend, and pretend; or believe lies about myself and the other. Love resists and repels evil. It covers over. It heaps burning coals. It never fails. Being perfect like the Father means choosing to let love win, every time.

I generally feel like people are out to take from me. Jesus says, *let them take. I have given everything for you and will keep giving, keep restoring, keep protecting. Let me love you. Let me fill you. Let me be enough.*

> Whoever does not love abides in death...By this we know love, that he laid down his life for us, and we ought to lay down our lives for the brothers... Little children, let us not love in word or talk but in deed and in truth.[66]

I can let go of justice, vengeance, control, self-preservation. I can cling to love and his name as a safe place. I can be stripped of every external thing I have because of the garden within, the secret abundance of care and decadent love. The Kingdom of God is within me. It is kept safe there. Nothing can separate me from the love of God. I can embrace an enemy of love with the love within: *I am lovely. I am loved. And*

---

64 I Corinthians 13:4-7
65 James 4:7
66 I John 3:14, 16, 18

you are, too. I will carry your burden of unlove, so you can know this love I know. I will let you strip me down, so you can find the treasure within.

There are other ways to fight enemies, but love is the only way to *win.*

In the presence of my enemies

This side of paradise, there will always be enemies, within and without. We fight the human ones with love and the non-human ones with spiritual authority. The strong man is bound and the stronger man's Spirit is living in us and loving us. It may not seem like love is winning in this world. It may not seem profitable or safe to choose love when most people are not choosing it. But choosing love is the way of the garden. I think of Jesus choosing love, even to the death. He could have chosen a different kind of power to defeat his enemies, but it would have ultimately backfired. When Judas came for Jesus at Gethsemane, he came armed with a mob wielding swords and clubs. As mentioned before, when Peter took out his sword and used it, Jesus said to him:

> Put your sword back into its place. For all who take the sword will perish by the sword. Do you think that I cannot appeal to my Father, and he will at once send me more than twelve legions of angels? But how then should the Scriptures be fulfilled, that it must be so?[67]

A legion is in the thousands, so twelve of them might be fifty thousand angels! Although physical retaliation could have flattened this little skirmish, it would have been like bowing to Satan and gaining the world but losing his soul. The Scriptures say Jesus is the Lamb of God who came to take away the sins of the world, so that those who believe can be with him in the *next* world. The *perfect* world. It had to be the garden of Gethsemane before the garden of paradise. Jesus told Pilate before His crucifixion,

> "My kingdom is not of this world. If my kingdom were of this world, my servants would have been fighting, that I might not be delivered over to the Jews. But my kingdom is not from the world."[68]

These were physical enemies, and Jesus was fighting them with love. He knew the Father's desire for him and for us, so he stuck to the plan out of love for his Father

---

67 Matthew 26:52-54
68 John 18:36

and love for the ones who would believe and receive this righteous sacrifice as *their* righteousness. The table set before him was the garden of his Father's love and provision. Jesus was surrounded by brutal enemies, and the Father was so pleased with him for choosing love. If Jesus could just keep trusting that this was so and keep choosing the Father's will over his own, love was going to win against *every* enemy! For good! Forever!

It is really hard to trust God when surrounded by enemies, especially since we live in the presence of enemies. So, can we live in the presence of God at the same time? Does the existence of enemies cancel out the existence of God, or, at least, the *goodness* of God?

Enemies represent and rouse fear in us: fear of pain and death and loss. Jesus' friend John wrote that perfect love drives out fear.[69] God is inviting us into the garden of his perfect love. Although good and evil can co-exist, in the sense that God's Holy Spirit can live in our hearts while we live in a world contaminated by evil, love and fear cannot co-exist inside of us. If God's love isn't driving out our fears, then our fears are driving out his love.

One late November evening, I was driving on the expressway with my boys, nine and seven, when I hit some black ice and lost control of my Jeep. We slid and swerved on the icy road, then careened sideways into the grassy embankment with a jolt and a roll. The Jeep flipped over and came to a stop, driver's side up. It happened really fast but felt like slow motion. I remember my expletive, my fear, the crunch of metal and glass, the pull of my seat belt as I hung from the roof, the silence of my boys in the back seat. When we came to a stop, the radio was still playing. Gabe and I were suspended.

"Are you boys ok?" I asked.

"Yes."

"Don't unbuckle yet."

"I already did," Gabe said.

"I'm scared," Jaben said.

"I'm scared, too," I told him.

---

69 I John 4:18

It was so dark in the car and I couldn't get my bearings. I unbuckled, fumbled my way to a standing position and stuck my head out of the driver's side window. I could only see headlights barreling down I-94, illuminating the falling snow. We were out of the way of oncoming traffic and safe from more impact, unless a car hit the ice the same way we did. I pulled my head back in and saw my glasses hanging by one arm from the driver's side window. "Oh, my glasses," I said. And put them on. Within a minute or so, a car had stopped and two young men ran over to my overturned Jeep.

"How many are in the car?" the one man asked. "Is anyone hurt?"

"My two boys and I are in here, and we are all ok," I said.

Then more people stopped and started coming to our aid. Someone let me use a phone to call Christoph. Then a man told me to turn away while he busted out the remaining glass in the window. He threw a coat over the window and reached for my boys to help them out. I, too, needed strong arms to lift me down to the ground. Others were looking for my possessions along the embankment. One man brought me my Pt. Pelee National Park pass that he had found in the snowy grass. Someone climbed in the Jeep and took my keys out of the ignition, found my phone and little backpack with my wallet in it and gave them to me. Others brought blankets out of their cars and wrapped my boys in them. One woman came running down from her house beyond the expressway. She had seen the Jeep flip from her house window and came to see if we were ok. She had come so quickly, she had forgotten her coat. I hugged her and told her we were ok.

A firetruck arrived. My husband arrived. Then a state trooper, a tow truck, and even an ambulance. The good people who had helped us got back into their cars and headed to their destinations, insisting that the boys keep the blankets. We got into Christoph's old Caddy and made it to home group with half of the carryout I had picked up before the accident. The other half had catapulted out of the Jeep. My boys were ok. I had only lost my Jeep. And my confidence.

In the days that followed, fear and love battled inside of me. It was clearer than ever to me that my control was limited; that my love for my boys could not protect them from my Jeep flipping; that being at the wheel with a valid driver's license did not mean I could navigate black ice. Powers much stronger than I were at work, and my question was, were they good or bad powers? Or if both, who was winning? Was I safe? Were my boys safe? Could I ever be sure?

I wanted to retreat for a while. Not drive. Not leave the house. Not make decisions. Because they may turn out to be unsafe decisions. The boys, on the other hand, were not shaken in their confidence or my competence. Gabe said it had been better than a roller coaster ride. Two days later, we drove Christoph to the airport in his Cadillac, because he was heading to Europe for a business trip. As we left the terminal, we passed a stretch of grass that sloped down to another road below us. Gabe said, "Maybe we could flip the Caddy down that hill." For our next stunt. It struck me that my boys still felt safe with me. Danger could not touch them, as long as we were together. I knew now, more than ever, that this was not entirely true, but because they believed it, my love for them conquered their fears.

My fears, on the other hand, were right at the surface. I had been trusting in *me* to get us safely through this journey. And now I felt completely untrustworthy and vulnerable to danger. The world was unsafe. Not just for other people, but for me and my children, too. Whom could I trust? Was God good? It was back to the garden again, and I was on the outside, looking in. God's love for me was not conquering my fears. From where I stood, I could see that God had been in it with us. When we slid, there was no one to slide into. With concrete walls and bridges everywhere, we regained friction on a grassy incline. We had room to roll(er coaster). I am not a physics superstar, but it was clear to me that my glasses would not have gingerly perched themselves by one arm on the window ledge. *Someone* had retrieved them for me and hung them in the only place that I, in the darkness and my nearsightedness, could have seen them. We flipped right before our Livernois exit—minutes from home and yet strangers on the side of I-94. The people who came to our aid, from the drivers who pulled over in the snowy darkness to the woman who ran out of her house and across the exit ramp to see if we were ok, treated us like family. Even in the dark and in my shock, I could see their faces—some lighter, some darker—and hear their voices, some with accents. I felt like the disciples seeing Jesus in the upper room: "Now we know that you know all things and do not need anyone to question you."[70]

I flipped my Jeep, and God flipped stereotypes. He showed me his love through glasses-retrieving angels and beautiful strangers. He assembled a family of helpers from different races and different places the moment I was in need. Even in my shock and fear, I knew there was purpose in our being alive—God still wanted us here. He wanted love to win and his kingdom to come in our hearts.

> "Do you now believe? Behold, the hour is coming, indeed it has come, when you will be scattered, each to his own home, and will leave me alone. Yet I am not alone, for the Father is with me."[71]

70 John 16:30
71 John 16:31-32

I could not trust myself, but could I trust *him*? *Would* I trust him, come what may?

> Even though I walk through the valley of the shadow of death, I will fear no evil, for you are with me; your rod and your staff, they comfort me. You prepare a table before me in the presence of my enemies; you anoint my head with oil; my cup overflows.[72]

In this life, God does not prepare a literal table in the presence of our enemies, to eat from or hide under. One day, after he has defeated all his enemies (and ours), he *will* prepare a great banquet table and we will feast with him.[73] But here, it is the feast of his presence and the oil of his love. It is the garden growing in our hearts. It is love winning in the presence of fear.

The winter is past

The fourth Lily Group was about abiding. Staying close to Jesus. Making our home with him. We read from Song of Solomon 2:

> The voice of my beloved! Behold, he comes, leaping over the mountains, bounding over the hills...Behold, there he stands behind our wall, gazing through the windows, looking through the lattice. My beloved speaks and says to me: "Arise, my love, my beautiful one, and come away, for behold, the winter is past; the rain is over and gone. The flowers appear on the earth, the time of singing has come, and the voice of the turtledove is heard in our land."[74]

Winter is an enemy. It freezes life and kills growing things. It is dark. In my time alone with this passage at Lily Group, I thought about winters past. I thought about my friend who was tormented by anxiety and depression after her third child was born. I thought about the year after falling in love with Christoph, when we were separated by the Atlantic, my parents' marriage was ending, and everything was tumbling. But then I thought of *Jesus'* winter that is past. The winter of the cross. It means *my* winter of sin and separation from Jesus is past. He is saying to me, *'Arise my love, my beautiful one, and come away' from death and despair and barrenness and loneliness. Our love can bloom. We can sing. We can have beauty. We can have*

72 Psalm 23:4-5
73 Matthew 26:29; Revelation 19:6-9
74 Song of Solomon 2:8-13

growth. Come away. Set yourself apart. Say goodbye to winter. Say goodbye to your fearful ways of thinking and being. Come with me into love. Come with me into the garden. Cling to me.

When we came back together as a group, we talked about the expectations people have of us and the expectations we have of ourselves. Kate shared a recent dream where she was talking on the phone with a friend from college and wanted to be done with the conversation but felt she had to say something helpful and profound. Liz talked about putting up walls to protect herself from the things she fears. And it made me think of the bridegroom in Song of Solomon coming to the wall and looking through the window. He does not break the wall down or pound on the window. He says, "Arise, my love, my beautiful one, come away with me." He puts his desire out there, but he does not force his way. Love cannot be forced. It must be chosen. He will not compromise love to get to us. Far from sitting on his hands, God has emptied himself, stretched out his hands to have and to hold us, but he will not coerce us into being with him.

If we open ourselves to his desire for us, it changes everything: how we love, how we lead, how we parent, how we think. But we cannot love him and be loved by him behind walls of fear. We have to leave those walls behind and come away with him into the garden, where our hearts can heal and bloom. Although his love protects us from fear, it does not protect us from pain and the presence of enemies. The darkness and death shadows are real, but so is his glorious light and final victory. And that's what we need to remember. It is finished. The winter is past.

Speaking the truth in love,
we are to grow up in every way
into him who is the head,
into Christ from whom the
whole body joined and held
together by every joint
with which it is equipped when
each part is working properly,
makes the body grow so that
it builds itself up in love.

Ephesians 4:15-16

BODY REALITY

Stained glass window, St. Anne's Church, Detroit 2009

Church

The church I grew up in was the village that raised me. My parents sang in a quartet from my infancy, and at their rehearsals, I played hide and seek under the wooden pews and spaceship in the frosted glass alcoves around the sanctuary. I had freedom at church to be creative and involved. I wrote and directed a puppet play of the story of Esther. At Neighborhood Bible Camp, my friends and I helped with games and put on bathrobes and sandals and acted out Bible stories for the younger kids. In junior high and high school, we took trips to music festivals and white-water rafting rivers. For several years, we had a youth choir and performed musicals. I loved the mission conferences in February, where missionaries would come and speak about the countries they were living in and what they did there. I loved the Wednesday night service before Thanksgiving, where people could stand up and share what they were thankful for, and every year, my grandpa stood up and wept at God's goodness.

Church for me was structure and community and recreation. God was real. I belonged. It was all that I needed as a kid. When I entered adolescence, I needed more. I was good at being a kid, and I didn't question myself or others very much. But when I started changing from a kid into a woman, I lost my confidence. I did not like what was happening to me in the mirror. I had no sense of style. I did not know what to do with hairspray. I did not like what was happening to my heart. It hoped for so much and broke so easily. I did not like what was happening to my words. They used to command and joke and recite and defend, and now they only threw barbs, when I really needed them to ask for a listener. One Friday night when I was thirteen, my parents and siblings went bowling and I stayed home at the piano, playing minor chords until these words came out:

Don't touch me
I'm alright
I'll handle it on my own
Don't help me
It's my fight
I'll struggle alone
The walls are closing in
His light is fading
I'm dying from within
So tired of masquerading
Please don't bother to love me

I'm not worth anyone's time
No need to listen, no need to care
Stay away, stay away
Leave me to wallow in my pain
I'm alone, and I'm to blame
Stay away

I never intended for anyone to see those words, but then I accidentally left them at the piano, and my mom found them. She came into my room, holding the incriminating piece of paper. "What's this?" she asked. I couldn't tell if she were sad or angry. I felt exposed and afraid, but also a little hopeful.

"Just something I wrote," I said, staring at my desk.

"How could you write something like this?" she asked.

I think it was genuinely unfathomable to her that her daughter could write, let alone *feel*, something so dark. She took it personally. I felt like I had done something wrong. "I don't know," I said.

I took the paper and put it on my desk. She might have been near tears. I had the thought of trying to console her or lessen the blow, but I said nothing. Then she walked away, and I closed the door to my room. My song had come true. I could say that she felt shut out of my life—that I had convinced her I didn't need her. I could also say that she was my mommy, and if she only would have embraced me at that moment and wept for my pain, I may have melted in her arms and something in me may have been healed. As it was, the moment that almost brought us together passed unredeemed and left us on the outside of each other.

When I was sixteen, I told my dad that I was unhappy at home. I remember him slamming his fist onto my bed and asking, "How can you *say* that?" He took it personally. He gave me everything he knew to give; he went to all of my competitions and performances. I did not know the first thing about unhappiness, he said. He walked out angry, perplexed, a lot like my mom had walked out several years earlier after discovering my song lyrics.

By the time I went away to college, I had been emotionally living on my own for some time. During my first week in Ann Arbor, there was a resource fair in my dorm, and I signed up for more information about Christian Life Church. It was a student church with a volunteer pastor that held Sunday services across the street in the School of

Education. A few days later, I got a call from George, who worked at the church. He invited me to a dinner for international students, because he had heard that I had worked with refugees the previous summer. After that, we hung out pretty regularly. I think it was part of his job to hang out with new students, and I liked the attention and his company. When we hung out at Espresso Royale, the ordering part was easy. He ordered a Café Au Lait, and I got a Mocha Java. When our drinks were ready, we sat down across from each other. "How are you?" he asked.

That's when it started getting challenging. How was I to answer? At home, sharing who I really was and how I really felt had caused confusion and abandonment. My mind raced to think of something impressive to share each time he asked. Eventually, I came to trust George's motives and his friendship. But I did not look at him or tell him the whole truth.

That February, George organized a spring break trip to St. Petersburg, Florida. We stayed at a church a couple of blocks from the Gulf. I was with some of the best people I had ever met. We put on miniature plays for one another in the sanctuary, utilized the dark and remote corners of the church for games of *sardines*, danced around with grapefruits while preparing meals, engaged in water gun fights (I had a hose connected to my gun that shot water from my forehead), and congregated in Sunday School rooms for special events, such as laying on our stomachs and lapping up apple juice out of Styrofoam bowls (we couldn't find cups) or simulating a call-in radio show using our feet as telephones.

When I had had enough of laughter and people, I retreated upstairs to the nursery or to the choir room. The choir room was connected to the nursery, which had once been something else, because there was a stage at one end with doors on either end of the stage. The doors led to a kind of backstage room with racks of choir robes and choir music and a piano. It was my secret room. Sometimes I played the piano and sang. Sometimes I sat on the floor and let myself be sad. No one ever found me there. I wanted to share the room and my sadness with someone, but I feared it would go badly. One night, I went up to the nursery and wrote in my journal:

> When I cry, I cry alone. Still. I do not reach out when I need. I run, run as fast as I can. Laugh loud. Tell more jokes. I don't know how to be weak. I don't know where to start.

As I sat there alone on the edge of tears, George walked in. He tried to start up a conversation, but I was working so hard at holding everything in that I only parted my lips enough to let out a couple of monosyllables. He stopped trying and left. As the door closed behind him, I threw myself onto the blue nursery carpet and wept, because my insides hurt, and because I had missed my chance to not be alone.

A few minutes later, the door opened again. It was George. "I knew you were going to cry," he said. "That's why I left. And that's why I came back."

He gathered me up in his arms and let me blubber out the contents of my heart. It had been in there so long, it just came tumbling out. He looked into my puffy red eyes and listened to my deepest, darkest confession: "I'm just a loser..."

He asked if he could pray with me. He listened as I wept my brokenness to God. When it was his turn, his voice began to break. I opened my eyes to see my tough Puerto Rican friend face down, his body shaking with sobs, "God, why does everyone leave me?"

I had never seen him cry before. I knew nothing of the sadness he carried. I loved him for letting me see it.

When it was over and we were again facing each other—puffy, snot-covered, exhausted and free—George asked, "What now?" Part of me wanted to remain indefinitely with him in the nursery. I was afraid to leave him and the sacred moments we shared.

This was church.

We were church. We were Christ's *body,* and Christ was nourishing us and cherishing us in a space that had opened just wide enough to let love in. I was afraid to close back up.

"What now?" George asked.

"I don't know."

"You need to talk to someone; to one of the women here."

I left George and the nursery and went down to the parlor type room where the other girls had let loose their sleeping bags. I decided that I would talk to Melanie, who was in the School of Social Work and seemed the most able to receive a random disclosure. She was sitting on a couch, reading by lamplight. I asked her if I could talk to her in the morning. She said yes. With that arranged, I crawled in my sleeping bag and fell asleep. In the morning, Mel and I went for a walk in the warm Florida sunshine. We stopped at a low wall in a quiet neighborhood of palm trees and flowers and pastel colored houses and sat down. I don't know what I said, but I know that she listened quietly and seriously. And that was what I needed from her.

Known and loved

> To be loved but not known is comforting but superficial. To be known and not loved is our greatest fear. But to be fully known and truly loved is, well, a lot like being loved by God. It is what we need more than anything. It liberates us from pretense, humbles us out of our self-righteousness, and fortifies us for any difficulty life can throw at us.[75]

When I was a child, I felt appreciated for my involvement and contributions to the greater good. As an adolescent, I stopped believing I had much of value to contribute. As young womanhood was taking over my body and people's expectations of me, I grieved the carefree kid I was losing and felt ashamed of the unfeminine female I was becoming. It was a time of loss and unwanted exposure.

Jack Debuke said I walked like a gorilla. When he was in 6th grade and I was in 5th grade, and we were battling each other in snow wars at recess, I once picked up Jack and body-slammed him into a pile of snow. The next time he saw me, he said to one of his classmates, "Watch out for *her*. She's a tiger." But when he was in 8th grade and I was in 7th grade, he watched me walk past him into the choir room, and he said to one of his classmates, "Look at *her*. She walks like a gorilla." He slumped his shoulders, stuck his arms out a little from his sides, and moved his legs in a stiff swagger. This pierced me like an arrow. My face, however, revealed nothing. Only at home, alone in my bedroom, did I let the sadness press against my heart and leak out of my eyes, leaving puddles in my ears. It was the grief of the me I had lost and the me I had become. It was the heaviness of *dreaming*...for the courage to talk about my feelings, for friends that would receive me as I was, for a way of being that did not make people think of gorillas...and then *waking* to myself.

Adolescence is a dream exploding: if I am so obviously flawed, am I still valuable? If my parents are so obviously flawed, who will take care of me? What feels like annihilation is actually preparation for a deeper coming together, both physically and spiritually. But many of us tend to get stuck somewhere between leaving parents and finding God, which leaves us feeling abandoned by both. With time, we may recover from our adolescent awkwardness but not necessarily from the betrayal of abandonment or the shame of exposure. So, we hide behind an image of what we think God and others want from us, while our real selves remain unseen and untouched.

---

75 Keller, Tim. *The Meaning of Marriage: Facing the Complexities of Commitment with the Wisdom of God*. Penguin Books, 2013

In the first garden, Adam and Eve were naked and unashamed. They did not hate their own bodies. They were at peace with themselves and the God who made them. The three of them were fearless and intimate with one another. They trusted each other. Then Eve was tempted by the fear of missing out, and she and Adam stopped trusting God. That was when they lost him.

When Jesus entered the garden of Gethsemane, he was entering to find us again. He left his Father to find his bride, the church. He loved us to death. But his loving us is not enough to make us one with him. Love is a choice, and both sides have to choose. Entering the garden with him means leaving adolescence behind and trusting him enough to be *fully known* and *truly loved* by him and his body.

Learning to trust

By the time I met George in college, I had recovered quite a bit from adolescence on the outside. I was performing pretty well and feeling likable again, but I didn't feel lovable. George helped me believe that it was possible to be fully known and truly loved, but I needed (still need) a lot of assurance. As a teenager, I was mouthy, self-conscious, suspicious, pretending not to care, caring so much it ached, passionate, standoffish, full of shame, quick to blame. In a word: erratic. I am finding that getting older does not mature the teenager in my head. As soon as I stop believing that I am known and loved, I start behaving like that teenager again. I start flailing at the mouth, saying things I don't mean, defending myself, hating myself, and grasping for the offended pieces of myself, as I back into a corner of shame and isolation. My lack of trust is volatile like that. Other people's lack of trust is perhaps subtler. Like constipation. A fixed smile with uneasy eyes. A stiffness. An aloofness. An inability to get comfortable or let go.

After that night in the nursery, I wanted to stay on the inside of love. But college isn't an easy place for a loser to come clean. It is a place of smooth surfaces, where people look and act smart—except when they're drunk. I had to reach below the surface. I had to go underground—to the basement practice rooms in East Quad. It was as easy as turning in my student ID at the front desk and being assigned an available room. It was as hard as walking down the stairs, through the subterranean halls, turning the key and opening the door. It was a dingy space—gray walls, faded carpet, uncovered pipes, a piano; sometimes a couple of folding chairs. There were no mirrors, no spectators. It was like an AA meeting, except that only God and I were in attendance, and God was not in recovery. I sat on the floor or on the piano bench, and I tried to tell the truth:

> God, I talked to George about my change of emotions toward him. I told him how I didn't want him to ever leave my side. And he told me that he loved me, that I was one of his best friends, the little sister he never had, but... I'm crying a lot. Not because I am surprised, but because I am still alone. I know I am changed, because I have cried without shame in his presence—many times since the night in the nursery. I know I am changed, because I have loved. It is good to cry freely and feel deeply. But now I am aching because of that love. I am aching because of what I have lost and what I long for.

Shortly after George told me he was resuming his engagement to his fiancée, I went home for the weekend to see family and friends. I told a friend who knew George, and he said, "I think this hurts you more than you'll ever let on. I'm sorry, Rach. I'm really sorry..." I cried, and he held me. That evening, I ate leftovers with my mom, and I talked to her about it. I cried tears of sadness in front of my mom for the first time. A couple of months later, my mom and I were having lunch together at the Broadway Deli, and I was crying again. She cried with me, because it hurt her to see me hurting. It began sinking in to me that people were not keeping their distance from me at all, but rather I was the one always running ahead or lagging behind—never standing next to anyone for very long. When my mom walked away from me and my *don't touch me* song six years earlier, she was just respecting my wishes. When my dad got angry at my outburst of unhappiness, it was because he was giving me everything he knew how to give, everything I knew how to ask for.

> I've walked this life alone for many days
> I wave to the people passing by as we go our separate ways
> I keep walking so no one will see
> The frightened little girl inside of me
> With my head high and my heart broken
> I hold tightly to the words that have never been spoken
> And I keep walking
> Walking away from love

I first gave myself to my journals. I hired words as intermediaries. I hid behind my skin and filled pages with all that transpired underneath the smooth surface. Then I wrote letters to people I had met in different places, sending words to represent me. They represented me so beautifully that the bearers of my letters barely recognized me when they were with the rough draft of me in person. Then there was George and the night in the nursery, when everything under my skin came blubbering out in front of him. This was my first face-to-face glimpse at love. What allowed me this peek at the thing I craved was a loss of control in his presence. It was so messy and frightening that I did not have the courage to choose it. But when it came to me by surprise, I knew: this was the inside.

I remember my dad once singing Bette Midler's song to me: "Did you ever know that you're my hero, and everything I would like to be..." I think he meant it. Part of me wanted to be his hero—the fulfillment of his unfulfilled dreams, his unfulfilled self. I was divided. Should I work harder at maintaining control or harder at losing it?

> What have I left behind?
> Nothing I can't find
> In a novel or somewhere on TV
> Where the girl finds the man of her dreams
> And they hold each other and smile
> Because they know
> That they will be together forever
> My heart is warmed
> And I feel the tears rolling down my face
> I smile through them
> At the imaginary love
> Of two imaginary people

My college attempts at being part of Christ's body were twitchy with bravado and unbelief. My friend Jeffrey and I thought up *The Hillside Arsonists*[76] one night at a coffee shop. We had been in *The Upper Room* together the year before. It was a weekly gathering of about ten students in a second story apartment. We huddled together, enjoying each other and what we knew of Jesus and waited for instructions on what to do next. There was usually some silliness at first, like Head Moose, where everyone sits in a circle and has an animal motion and you do your animal motion and someone else's animal motion, and you try to become Head Moose. And then we'd talk about something that Jesus said or did that was recorded in the Bible and what it meant for us. What *he* meant to us. Then we prayed. It was all kind of awkward and exciting and mysterious, like falling in love.

---

76 Matthew 5:14 "You are the light of the world. A city on a hill cannot be hidden."

For Jeffrey and me, becoming hillside arsonists was the next step. We wanted to be bright and obvious...*out* with our loyalty to Jesus and his message. Flaming Christians. Four of our friends joined us, and the six of us met once a week in an East Quad classroom to study the teachings of Jesus and once a week at the Student Union to talk to unsuspecting students about Jesus. We would select some fast food, find a table together, eat in a tense silence, pray, and then split up to find people to talk to. It was always very frightening for me. I was not one to ask people questions, not even easy ones with obvious answers. So, to go up to peers that I did not know and ask if I could talk to them about Jesus was nearly heart-stopping. On one such occasion, I went upstairs to the pay phones and called George. I said, "I am at the Union and I am trying to find someone to talk to, but I am really scared. I don't want to give up, though. Will you pray for me?" He did, and I went back downstairs and approached a girl who was sitting by herself, studying. We talked for about half an hour. I do not remember the content of those interactions—just the feelings of dread. It was like I was a new sales representative for a miracle cream or a protein powder. Except I was selling a *person*. I believed in the product. I had heard the testimonials since childhood. Still, I felt like a fraud, because I did not personally feel smoother or healthier or lovelier since subscribing to the miracle person. Madeleine L'Engle once wrote:

> Christians have given Christianity a bad name. They have let their lights flicker and grow dim. They have confused piosity with piety, smugness with joy. During the difficult period in which I was struggling through my 'cloud of unknowing' to return to the Church and to Christ, the largest thing which deterred me was that I saw so little clear light coming from those Christians who sought to bring me back to the fold.[77]

I would contend that, if these flickering people were anything like I was, they had *never* shone brightly from the inside. They had never even *experienced* the inside. They had maybe changed their clothes and beverages and some of their words, but they still lived on the outside of love. They had never learned to trust. Unfortunately, they were telling people that they were speaking from the inside, which made the inside seem like a drop off point for hypocrites and the deluded. I wanted it to be different with me. Jeffrey and I thought that by doing something crazy—like interrupting people while they were studying or hanging out with friends and proselytizing a little—we were getting closer to the inside. The desire for the inside motivated us to organize the Upper Room and the Hillside Arsonists. But fear and emotional ambivalence kept us from getting really close to it.

---

77 L'Engle, Madeleine. *Walking on Water: Reflections on Faith and Art.* Macmillan, 1995

I knew so few people on the inside. I knew of a few musicians, though, who had expressed longings for it. So, I gathered their songs around me, and it felt like being at a meeting. David Meece might share first.

> I've got this pain inside me. It speaks to me loud and clear. When there's so much to gain, there's always so much to lose.[78]

Then Bryan Duncan.

> I was raised with the lessons and the victory speech, and I fought for the standards that I could not reach. And I hold my tongue when the pain is great, and I cover my tears as we celebrate, while a private war rages with the fear and the doubt, as I try to run faster to find a way out.[79]

Margaret Becker might go next.

> I'm not gonna lie about feeling fine and knowing everything's okay. I just gotta believe that His hope inside will lead me to a better place. With every tear that I cry, I cling to the hope that will not die: He won't leave me here.[80]

I, too, would take my two cents and ten fingers to the practice room and put my confessions to music. Then one day I met Andi. She was a friend of George's. The day when things broke open between us was when I read her a paper I had written for my non-fiction class, entitled *Learning to Trust.* Then it was her turn to speak. Without flinching, she told me of being sexed by her father. And later her stepfather. It was the first of many meetings we had together. She let me see her and know her. We talked to God by candlelight. One evening, as she was telling me a sad story from her past, I started to cry. She wrapped her arms around me, and I held on to her thumbs, feeling like Pinocchio coming to life.

One Flesh

> For no one ever hated his own flesh but nourishes and cherishes it, just as Christ does the church, because we are members of his body. 'Therefore, a man shall leave his father and mother and hold fast to his wife, and the

---

78 Meece, David. "Learning to Trust." *Learning to Trust.* Star Song Records, 1992, CD.
79 Duncan, Bryan. "We All Need." *Anonymous Confessions of a Lunatic Friend.* Myrrh Records, 1990, CD.
80 Becker, Margaret. "I Will Not Lay Down." *Simple House.* Sparrow Records, 1991, CD

> two shall become one flesh.' This mystery is profound, and I am saying that it refers to Christ and the church.[81]

A friend asked me in an email about church, "Can we stop the performance and look at each other?" It's a question I am still trying to answer. The one you dress up for. The other undresses you. Are we ready for that kind of exposure?

I sat at the piano one Sunday morning, playing chords and trying to pray. I wore my worship like an apron of hospitality, tied with resentment and splotchy with martyr sauce. I waited on God like he was my next customer: "What do you need, sir?" I felt his Spirit whisper back, *What do you need, Rach?* God was looking at me. Affectionately. His kindness brought me to tears and untied my apron strings. I let him nourish me with his love.

Another time at the piano preparing to worship, my spirit was willing, but my flesh was tense and tired with the cares of the day. I got up from the piano and slid onto the couch to listen, and I felt the Spirit whispering, *Let me hold you. Let me be strong for you and take care of you.* Yes, Lord. The tears came again and brought with them a willingness to rest and get quiet and trust.[82] He was the song I had been trying to sing.[83]

I cry a lot with him these days, because we are looking at each other more. I used to fight through my grief or hold it captive in my throat, so as not to attract vultures. I averted my eyes and chose performance over intimacy, settling for meeting needs and faking worship, instead of opening myself to the profound mystery. More and more, though, I'm learning to look past enemies into the eyes of love and find myself *in Christ*, one with his crucified flesh and perfection, my cares in a heap on the floor.

When we are in performance mode, it can feel like everybody wants a piece of us. But God doesn't want a piece of us. He looks right at us and waits to have and to hold us. Sometimes I wonder why he waits. What if we never get there? I think of Martha welcoming Jesus into her home but then feeling left out.[84] "Lord, do you not care that my sister has left me to serve alone? Tell her then to help me." Maybe Martha would have been fine if Mary were serving in the kitchen with her. But Mary was listening at the feet of Jesus. What woman *does* that? Contempt came rushing in to snuff out Martha's desire. *Mary is being selfish. Lord, don't you care?*[85]

---

81 Ephesians 5:29-32
82 Isaiah 30:15
83 Psalm 118:14
84 Luke 10:38-42
85 Mark 4:38

> "Martha, Martha, you are anxious and troubled about many things, but one thing is necessary. Mary has chosen the good portion, which will not be taken away from her."

Jesus gave Martha permission to listen. The Greek word for obedience means, "submission to what is heard."[86] Mary was listening, and Martha could, too. It was the only way to know the one she was serving. It was the only way to know what he thought of her and what he dreamed for her. It was the only way to know who he was and what pleased him. Listening is the first part of obedience. When Mary chose to listen to Jesus, she was choosing to give him her attention before her service, since knowing him would shape how she served him. Maybe she made the best *Dolma* around, but in listening to Jesus, she found out he didn't like stuffed onions, so the next time he was over she and Martha made lentil soup. Or maybe Mary cooked. And Martha listened. To love Jesus well is to listen to him well, because if we listen well, it changes us.

This chapter is a tough one for me to write, because, on the one hand, I have church wounds, and on the other, God has so much beauty for his bride, beyond what I can ask or imagine. I am struggling to describe what it means to be one with each other and with Christ, because it IS a profound mystery. I know oneness takes trust, and I don't trust well. So, I feel kind of fraudulent dreaming up a solution when I am a part of the problem. Remember when I wrote that as I got older, I needed more from the church than structure and community and recreation? I needed the whole me to be known and loved, but I didn't believe it was possible, so I didn't let anyone close enough to know me. And I didn't try to know other people either, in case they were feeling as scared about exposure as I was. It is a lack of trust that keeps us from being one flesh. It may look like a division in culture or language or race or doctrine, but it is more deeply about trust. If we do not trust each other, we cannot love each other. Because love always trusts. And if we do not love each other, then it is not safe to be known. To love each other well is to listen well and be changed by what we hear.

Everything I needed to know about sex I learned from my husband. And vice versa. Hallelujah. We are lifelong learners. Still, it isn't easy to be one with him—not because I don't read Cosmopolitan, but because I am afraid to trust. He is telling me I am beautiful. I am safe with him. He is telling me that he wants me, just like this. Can I trust him enough to lose myself in how he feels about me? I see the same struggle with Christ and the church. Can we trust Christ enough to listen to him and submit to what we hear? Can we entrust each other with how human we are, so he can make us as holy as he is? It will take a lot of listening to him and to each other. It will be messy, unpredictable and uncontainable. We might cry out with loud cries and tears before the weight of the world slides off our shoulders and we go light and heavy with glory.

86 "Obedience." *Strong's Exhaustive Concordance: New American Standard Bible*, updated ed., Lockman Foundation, 1995. *Bible Study Tools Online*, www.biblestudytools.com/concordances/strongs-exhaustive-concordance/.

Coming close to Jesus

> I appeal to you therefore, brothers and sisters, by the mercies of God, to present your bodies as a living sacrifice, holy and acceptable to God, which is your spiritual worship.[87]

Coming to God as we are is an act of trust and the purest worship we can offer. We don't have righteousness to offer God. All we can give him is ourselves, trusting that he wants us and he is good. Jesus says, "Come to me, all who labor and are heavy laden, and I will give you rest."[88] And I desperately want to rest in him. But trust is an abyss. A garden of tears. A churning sea. Do I dare enter? Defy gravity? Is his love big enough to hold me up and bring me out of fear? We each have to decide this, personally and not abstractly. Or else we will sing the songs and agree with the sermons about the Good Shepherd who takes care of his sheep but not really believe it enough to let him lead us. The only way to make it personal is to risk coming close.

There's a woman in the Bible who scandalized a Pharisee's dinner party with her tears and her worship[89]. Where the story picks up, she is already in the process of coming close to Jesus, but she is described as *a woman of that town, who was a sinner.* Her reality is out there and heavy on her, and she wants to lose herself in the reality of Jesus. Maybe she heard how he had compassion on a widow who was weeping over her lost son; how he touched a burial stretcher, though it was considered unclean; how he gave the widow back her son from the dead, just by saying, "Get up!"[90] and she was ready to be his next miracle. So, she came—uninvited by the Pharisee but invited by Jesus. Despite the negative voices in her head and the bad people in her past, she believed that Jesus was speaking to her, and that he meant what he said. She received his invitation to come close.

> As she stood behind Jesus at his feet, weeping, she began to wet his feet with her tears. She wiped them with her hair, kissed them, and anointed them with the perfumed oil. Now when the Pharisee who had invited him saw this he said to himself, "If this man were a prophet, he would know who and what kind of woman this is who is touching him, that she is a sinner."

87 Romans 12:1
88 Mathew 11:28
89 Luke 7:36-50
90 Luke 7:11-15

The woman came close, and Simon kept his distance. Simon needed forgiveness as much as the next person; it just wasn't obvious to him or the company he kept. I believe he put a lot of energy into image and keeping his need for forgiveness hidden. He wanted *some* contact with Jesus, but he did not want to give up control. Jesus had invited him to come close, but Simon wanted the relationship on his terms. *How about if I just invite Jesus over for dinner? I will make the guest list and plan the menu. I will make it nice. There will be no alcohol. No tax collectors. No needy crowds. No kisses. No feet touching. No smeary oil. No messes.*

Simon had insulated himself from his own desperation and from the reality of Jesus. He thought to himself, *if this man were a prophet, he would know what kind of woman is touching him, that she is a sinner.* He shaped his interpretation of what was going on to match the reality that was most comfortable to him, which was: Jesus is not a prophet, the woman is a sinner, and he, well, he isn't going to say or do anything to incriminate himself. (Too bad Jesus could read his thoughts).

The woman believed Jesus. She received his offer of rest for her weary, used up body and soul. She came close to him with her jar of alabaster, her gift of gratitude. She came to him in openness, trusting that he would protect her. When she came close to him with her defenses down, she started to weep. And then, with her hair, she wiped his feet that she had bathed in tears. She kissed his feet and poured her perfumed oil on them. She gave herself to him. She touched him because she wanted to, because she loved him, because he had invited her into his rest. This must have been painful as well as healing—to make intimate contact with herself and with Jesus. In those moments, Jesus was redeeming her body and her spirit.

> Then Jesus said to her, "Your sins are forgiven." But those who were at the table with him began to say among themselves, "Who is this, who even forgives sins?" He said to the woman, "Your faith has saved you; go in peace."[91]

Jesus and that woman knew how to be church together. Simon wanted a nice planned event. The woman wanted Jesus. She grieved and she worshiped. Jesus forgave her, redeemed her and anointed her with peace. They gave each other the best that they had, and it made them one.

91 Matthew 7:48-50, New International Version

Coming Close to One Another

Therefore, confess your sins to one another and pray for one another, that you may be healed.[92]

Submit to one another out of reverence for Christ.[93]

Confession and submission are signs of trust and the way into oneness with Jesus and others. Jesus showed us how to come close to one another in submission. He scandalized a dinner party, too, when he took off his outer garments and washed his friends' feet before the Passover meal. The crazy part wasn't the foot washing, because that was customary. Peter objected because Jesus was their *teacher*, and he was doing the dirty work left to *servants*. But submission knows no hierarchy, and without it, there's no oneness. Jesus said to Peter, "Unless I wash you, you have no part with me."[94] And to all of his friends, he said, "If I then, your Lord and Teacher, have washed your feet, you also ought to wash one another's feet."[95] When we come close to Jesus, he touches our broken places and washes us with the truth of his love for us.[96] He frees us to know and be known, to love and be loved, to give and receive care and confession. There is submission involved in both serving and being served. On both sides, it is a stripping down of pretense and risking exposure. Fear bullies us into hiding behind an image of good enough and big enough. Love gives us courage to out ourselves and get smaller.

Confession is coming to each other with dirty feet. Once, I shared something Kate had told me in confidence, and the awareness of my betrayal started burning in me. She and I had spent time together in the Lily Group and on Wednesday mornings coming close to Jesus with our confessions, but now my confession was personal. My sin was against *her*. I called her on the phone and spoke in confessional ambiguities. Kate was gracious, but I knew there was more to tell. It wasn't over—my confession or her reaction to it. I would tell her in the morning, when we met to worship and pray.

This thing between us kept us both awake that night. I was struggling because I had caused a rift, and my saying more might widen it. I couldn't *not* say it. I couldn't worship and pray without coming clean. But the act of confessing, though a catalyst for reconciliation, might first cause distance, and I hated that. I couldn't fix what I

92 James 5:16
93 Ephesians 5:21, New International Version
94 John 13:8
95 John 13:14
96 Ephesians 5:26

had broken. I couldn't determine how she would respond or how long the woundedness would keep her from trusting me. In the night, I heard the Proverb in my head, *A gossip separates close friends.*[97] The realization of my gossip power to separate me from my friend was aching in me.

Kate couldn't sleep because she was wrestling with my humanness. I wasn't enough. I let her down. And would again. I wasn't always safe. I was a risk. Was I worth it? Could she ever trust me again? She told me that she wanted to be able to tell me anything, but if I was not going to keep it safe, what should she tell and not tell?

No one else came that morning to worship and pray. God was protecting our reconciling space. I told her exactly what I had said to another that wasn't mine to tell. She reached her hand toward me. I took it and started sobbing. She started reading Scriptures about a withered fig tree and faith and forgiveness. She looked at me and said, "I forgive you, Rachael." I knew it was so. But the damage and the broken pieces remained. I prayed that God would heal the wounds that I had caused.

Kate did not hold back her wrestling from me. She let me hear her heart as she exposed it to God. She wanted love to win, but she was scared. She didn't trust herself or me. "I don't want to be a garden locked up," she cried. I asked her if I could play something at the piano, and she said yes. It at first felt awkward to play and sing with our realities out there and heavy on us. But as we offered Jesus our broken spirits,[98] he took them and blessed us with the reality of him. *Your sins are forgiven. Your faith has saved you. Go in peace.*

In order to be loved fearless, we have to keep exposing our fears to love. The enemy tends to strike with a one-two punch: He tempts us and then shames us. He gives us a tempting thought and then he tells us we're stupid for being tempted like that. He has done this to me so many times. Even now, the enemy is trying to keep us from coming close to each other. He wants us to stick with body image. He wants us to profess and act like we are healed even when sin is rotting out our insides. Jesus says, that's not healing. That's a tombstone.[99] To be healed, we confess our sins to each other and pray for each other. So, I'll tell you about one of my stupid temptations. Once, after a mountaintop weekend with Jesus and some friends, I started to fear as soon as the weekend was coming to an end. (Why couldn't we just pitch our tents up there a while longer?) Some of these friends were planning Bible times and barbecues together, and I wasn't a part of those plans. The devil knows my fears. He

---

97 Proverbs 16:28
98 Psalm 51:17
99 Matthew 23:27

feeds them to me on a regular basis, and I usually swallow them, even though they give me heartburn and start devouring me from the inside out. *No one has time for your petty hurts and fears, Rach. You can care for others, but nobody's gonna care for you. You can be strong for others, but nobody's gonna be strong for you when you're weak, so don't bother.* No, I don't want to believe this. I'll tell Kate how I'm feeling. The lion roared back, *You were just with her. Give her a break. Besides, if she's not feeling what you're feeling, why expose yourself and burden her with your sadness?*

I couldn't shake the lies or the fear on my own. I called Kate and talked to her voicemail. And cried. And fought through the contempt. And exposed my sad and fearful heart. And hung up.

Immediately, the fear fell off. But the sadness lingered.

Liz had sent me a link to Jason Upton's *Whisper* song that morning, so I sat down and listened.

> When my faith is prone to fear, remind me of your love. Remind me that you never let me go. Remind me. Remind me. Remind me of your love.[100]

I thanked her in a text, and confessed my earlier fear of not knowing where I belong and feeling left behind. Liz said she would pray for me and confessed some of her own fears. Strength and courage moved into my heart where fear had vacated.

Later that afternoon, I got this text from Kate:

> Hi friend that I love so much. Thank you for calling and confessing and being real. I'm glad the fear fled! And I want to hear more about the sadness if/when you have more to say about it...not so I can fix it but so I can be alongside you in it. Cuz that's where I want to be.

Confession and a couple of friends to receive it were what it took to resist the devil and get love winning again. It seems so small in the grand scheme, but it changed my whole thought process, and, consequently, the whole course of my emotions and actions in the days to come. Fear is a prophet, even if a false one. Fears come true, if we believe in them more than we believe in love. Exposing my heart to the right people, though it felt risky, brought me back to the truth: God is taking care of me at

---

100 Jason Upton. "Whisper". Upton, Jason. *A Table Full of Strangers, Vol. 1.* Jason Upton, 2015

every turn. And he has given me good friends (with fears of their own to confess) on the journey, who can handle my confessions. I needed this assurance.

This is a profound mystery, but God made us to be one with him and each other. As we come near to one another in humility, gentleness and patience, we preserve the oneness we were called to.

And they were bringing children
to him that he might touch them,
and the disciples rebuked them.
But when Jesus saw it, he was
indignant and said to them,
'Let the children come to me;
do not hinder them, for to such
belongs the kingdom of God.
Truly, I say to you, whoever does
not receive the kingdom of God
like a child shall not enter it.'
And he took them in his arms and
blessed them, laying his hands on them.

Mark 10:13-16

Parents and Children

Gabe biking the RiverWalk (with found plastic bag on a string), Detroit 2014

Growing up into a kid

Psychologist Erik Erikson[101] theorized that, throughout our development, we are faced with a series of identity crises. An infant's crisis is trust vs. mistrust: *Can I trust the world?* A baby's world is usually centered on its mother. If the mother is dependable and provides touch and food and care, then the world is a safe place. As babies grow into little children, trust is challenged in more personal ways: *Is it ok to be me in this world? Is it ok to like what I like and do what I do?* This is further challenged in adolescence, as the child transitioning into adulthood tries to reconcile the person he or she is becoming with the person he or she is *expected* to become. The internalizing of expectations is both arbitrary and rigid, in that an adolescent chooses whom to listen to and whom to believe, and these become the people who have the power to free or to kill. The crisis of early adulthood is intimacy vs. isolation: *Can I love and be loved*? If there is no reconciliation between who we are and who we think we are supposed to be, love loses. Fear (of being known and found wanting) wins. We stay stuck in adolescence. We get older but not less fearful. Our relationships stay superficial. We resign ourselves to emotional isolation.

The turning point spiritually is reconciling who we are with whom God expects us to become. This may sound ambitious and impossible, but the crazy thing is, God expects us to become kids. He expects us to receive his kingdom like children. When children are offered something they want, no matter how extravagant or ridiculous it is, they usually accept it. It could be a castle, a thousand gumballs, fairy dust, or a rocket ship — they will take it, if it's something that they want. They may not even say *thank you*. They probably won't wonder where it came from or concern themselves with paying for it.

Jesus is offering us his kingdom, and an adolescent response is, "Hmmm...I don't know..." He's offering to take us in his arms and bless us, but if we are stuck in adolescence, we hold back. We know better. We know...cruelty, disappointment, rejection...better. We know how it is in the real world. We're done with make believe. We know you have to prove yourself. You have to earn things. We know there are winners and losers. Mostly losers. We know deferred dreams. We have listened to the wrong voices.

My oldest son is eleven as I write this. He can do things with wires and circuits and electricity that I don't even know how to describe. He is playful and intense. He thinks deeply and talks freely. He loves cats. He loves his Nee Nees (I'd say they are blankets but they are much more to him than blankets). He loves to laugh and lead

101 Erikson, Erik. *Identity and the Life Cycle*. W. W. Norton & Company, Inc., 1994.

and learn and explore. He has always been this way. And he has been free to be himself. But this year, for the first time, it's not ok to be who he is at school. He's called names. He's not included. He's picked on and beat up on the bus. Adolescence is bullying him, threatening to steal his childhood. My boy feels uncool and doesn't like himself anymore. He struggles to trust those of us who like him. He struggles to believe anyone could. He is becoming wary of good gifts.

What is Jesus offering anyway? A treasure? A pearl? A wedding invitation? A seed? Is the offer any good? To get close enough to Jesus to answer these questions requires a growing down. Getting there is different for everyone, but we have to get to a place of trust in order to be led to Jesus, to be held in his arms, and to receive his blessing. Because what he is offering us is *himself.*

I've grown up a free agent. D.H. Lawrence wrote: Perhaps only people who are capable of real togetherness have that look of being alone in the universe. The others have a certain stickiness, they stick to the mass.[102] I have that capacity and that look. I have discovered that real togetherness is hard to come by. My love languages[103] are time and touch: *If you love me, you will spend time with me. If you love me, you will want to be close to me.* But I'm not the easiest person to spend time with or get close to. I have had moments of real togetherness. Like, with George in the church nursery. Or with Andi. At Lily Group. With my husband. But I've also had togetherness backfire. I *thought* I enjoyed real togetherness with a friend in college. We shared our hearts. We laughed and cried. We prayed together. Even after college, we made time for these things. One day, though, she called me and told me that being with me was stressful for her. She didn't want what I wanted. She didn't want me in her life anymore. This was such a hard and unexpected blow. I asked a pastor I trusted, am I a bully? Do I bully people into *real togetherness* with me? I thought this was a mutual friendship. She had told me that being with me was refreshing to her soul. But it seems the opposite was true. I started thinking, maybe I have that look of being alone in the universe because I really am. Maybe people tolerate me out of pity or fear, but they don't really *want* me. They don't really *love* me. This set me back into adolescence for a while.

When Kate and I started spending time together, we had a lot to learn about real togetherness. We were wary of being still and being known. Ashamed of empty-handedness. Afraid of losing control. But we took time. To *be.* To listen. To find each other. We sat outside in lounge chairs, letting the sun warm us. Letting the Son heal us. Feeling like treasures in a field being unearthed. I grew up believing that I had to be strong, even if no one was going to be strong for me. I had to take care of

102 Lawrence, D.H. *Lady Chatterly's Lover.* Bantam Classics, 1983
103 Chapman, Gary. *The Five Love Languages: the secret to love that lasts.* Northfield Publishing, 2009

others, even if no one was going to take care of me. These are the voices I listened to and the expectations I tried to fulfill. And they kept me from Jesus. But God used Kate to help me become *childlike*. I learned to trust her to be strong for me and to care for me, when I needed these things. And because I trusted her, I let her bring me to Jesus, so he could take me in his arms and bless me with new birth.

Leaving Home and Saying Goodbye

> Something new and shattering is breaking through into something old. Something is trying to be born. And if the new thing is going to be born, then the old thing is going to have to give way, and there is agony in the process as well as joy, just as there is agony in the womb as it labors and contracts to bring forth the new life.[104]

To grow up into children who feel at home in Jesus' arms, we have to leave the home(s) we grew up in. The authors of *Love is a Choice*[105] write about *leaving home and saying goodbye* as both a physical and an emotional leaving. The emotional leaving is a journey similar to Kuebler-Ross's stages of grief,[106] with shock and denial as first responses, followed by anger, magical thinking and depression. Minirth and Meier add sadness as a final release of grief. With gratitude, I borrow from their wisdom and will try to describe how I see it at work in my life and the lives of others on this journey.

The agony of growing up is letting go of wounds and dreams and expectations. The wounds are familiar, as are the people who inflicted them. We dream and desire because God made us so, and we look to the people who fed and clothed us to feed our dreams and keep us safe.

When I was growing up, we had dinner at my grandma's every Thursday. Her specialty was pot roast with squishy carrots and potatoes and apple sauce. We ate and laughed together and then watched TV or played cards. My parents gave me space to be my own person. They helped me go to college and study abroad. My mom packed me a lunch every day, even in high school, and wrote notes on my napkins. My dad pitched softballs to me in the front yard. My parents went to almost all of my events and performances to support me and cheer me on. They wanted Jesus for me. They took me places where I would be exposed to the Bible and people who believe so that I could have a chance to make Jesus my home.

---

104 Buechner, Frederick. *The Magnificent Defeat.* HarperOne, 1985
105 Hemfelt, R. et al. *Love is a Choice: Recovery for Codependent Relationships.* Thomas Nelson, 1991
106 Kuebler-Ross, Elisabeth. *On Death and Dying.* MacMillan, 1977

I get to keep these beautiful things about my family. They are not the things I have to say goodbye to. I took some non-beautiful things into my adulthood as well, though: insecurity around women, contempt for femininity, distrust of God (and everyone else), pride (*My way is best*), shame (*I'm a loser*), and rejection (*If people really get to know me, they won't like me*). And these things have not been good parents to me. They have threatened me with fear and isolation, even when I was with people and appeared to be functioning well. They have scolded me into emotional hiding, when all I wanted was to be known and loved. I am not saying my parents taught me these things, but these are the things I learned. And these beliefs have wounded me and the people in my life over and over again.

The first step into leaving is to acknowledge the wounds that we carry and perpetuate, which can awaken a fury inside. When my parents' marriage started breaking up, I blamed my father. I told him I forgave him. I wanted to. I started to. But my anger just kept building and building. I was angry at him for hurting my mom. I was angry at being so ill-equipped for life and love. I was angry at being lied to. I was angry that I had tried to be his hero. I had dreams at night of yelling at him and physically beating him. I woke up tense and terrified at the anger and violence in me. Denial can seem better than this. More peaceful. Less messy. But there can be no healing of wounds that are not acknowledged. After a while, anger exhausts itself and goes to bed. And doesn't want to get up. Why bother? What's the point? Everything's a mess, and there's no fixing it. There's no going back to the way things were and no clear path forward. Why move? Depression. Then there may be a period of magical thinking, or focusing intensely on something unrelated to grief, believing it will shorten the process or bring relief. Like a grief lotto: if I win or succeed at this, all my problems will be solved. It is a step out of depression but into a new form of denial that believes there is no more grieving to do.

There is no way out of the valley of leaving apart from releasing the deep sadness of loss. Denial does not accept the loss. Anger tries to control it. Depression tries not to feel it. Magical thinking tries to re-frame it. Sadness surrenders to it and says goodbye. It is a time of releasing parents from unmet expectations and releasing oneself from parents' expectations. It's feeling the wounds of childhood and then releasing parents and self from guilt. It is saying goodbye to an identity forged by these expectations and wounds.

Liz said at Lily Group that she had put so much energy into being the person she thought other people wanted her to be that she didn't know who she really was. She asked, "Where have I been all my life?" A big part of grieving the loss of self is going back home to the expectations we believe were ours to fulfill there. I recently talked to a woman in her forties who hadn't spoken to her parents for several years and believed she had already left home and said goodbye. But when her father contacted her, all the old dynamics were still there. Her father hadn't changed: he still didn't understand her, didn't listen to her, said hurtful things to her. And she hadn't stopped expecting him to be different: to validate her, to protect her, to be a safe place for her. She is still holding out for this. She is putting her heart on hold for this. Why won't he do this for her, *be* this for her, so she can heal and move on?

When I first listened to the audio cassette of *Love is a Choice* in college, the awareness of who I was becoming because of what I was believing slid into my soul like concrete. Love always trusts and has no need to control or manipulate, but I did not trust. Perfect love drives out fear, but I was terrified. I wanted to say goodbye to my fearful ways of thinking and being. I wanted to say goodbye to my parents' power to free me or kill me. But if I did, what would I have left? If I died to fear, how could I be sure that love would resurrect me?

Re-Parenting

> Blessed be the God and Father of our Lord Jesus Christ! According to his great mercy, he has caused us to be born again to a living hope through the resurrection of Jesus Christ from the dead, to an inheritance that is imperishable, undefiled, and unfading...[107]

The letting go of wounds and expectations makes room for something new to be born. We have dreams and desires, and who will feed them and keep them safe, if not our parents? Leaving home feels like a death. I think of the disciples saying, "Now we know, Jesus, that you came from God. Now we believe you." But when believing him felt threatening and foreign, they ran back home to what was familiar, because they didn't want to die. Leaving home is losing life (identity through our parents), in order to find it (identity in Christ). *We* are the new thing trying to be born. To grow up into God's children, we have to be re-parented. To make room for this new parenting, we have to let go of our parents as the ultimate life givers (and takers). Like Jesus before Pilate, we have to realize that our parents do not have the power to free us or kill us. We both answer to a higher power,[108] a trustworthy Father.

I think of Jesus leaving home when he was twelve. He stayed in Jerusalem without his parents knowing, so he could be in the temple and learn from the teachers. After three days, his parents finally found him.

---

107 I Peter 1:3-4
108 John 19:10-11

> And his mother said to him, "Son, why have you treated us so? Behold, your father and I have been searching for you in great distress." And he said to them, "Why were you looking for me? Did you not know that I must be in my Father's house?" And they did not understand the saying that he spoke to them. And he went down with them and came to Nazareth and was submissive to them. And his mother treasured up all these things in her heart.[109]

There was tension and misunderstanding between Jesus and his earthly parents, not because he didn't love them but because he didn't see them as the ultimate authority in his life. When he was an adult, a similar thing happened.

> A crowd was sitting around him, and they said to him, "Your mother and your brothers are outside, seeking you." And he answered them, "Who are my mother and my brothers?" And looking about at those who sat around him, he said, "Here are my mother and my brothers! For whoever does the will of God, he is my brother and sister and mother."[110]

Jesus' relationship with his Father in heaven shifted his family dynamics. He shared his Father's values and desires and felt most at home with others who did as well. He loved his biological mother. Before he was crucified, he made sure John would care for her in his absence.[111] But I wonder if she was really the one parenting him in the ways and will of God. She wasn't with the people surrounding him when he began his ministry. This makes me believe that those who spent time with him and cared about what he cared about were the ones Jesus considered family.

Confession and submission were the family values that mattered to him. I think of him taking off his outer garments and washing his friend's feet. *Know me and let me serve you.* He didn't say, I'm done being parented, and now I'm doing all the parenting. He said, *I have siblings here. And mothers, too. We are growing up into God's children together.* He tended to move around a lot, but he always had family with him.

> He went on through cities and villages, proclaiming and bringing the good news of the kingdom of God. And the twelve were with him, and also some women who had been healed of evil spirits and infirmities: Mary,

---

109 Luke 2:48-51
110 Mark 3:3
111 John 19:26-27

> called Magdalene, from whom seven demons had gone out, and Joanna, the wife of Chuza, Herod's household manager, and Susanna, and many others, who provided for them out of their means.[112]

They were the people who left home and said goodbye to grow up with him into children of the Father.

God has given us relationships with one another to help us find him. David said to the Lord, "You are he who took me from the womb; you made me trust you at my mother's breasts."[113] A woman and her baby start their relationship in total vulnerability and dependence. Giving birth and mothering have brought me to deep places of re-parenting where I've been too focused on life and love to be ashamed of the exposure. When Eliana was born, Christoph caught her and placed her in my arms. Should I try and feed her?" I asked. "You don't have to do anything," the nurse said. "She will find you." And sure enough, my just born waxy girl scooted herself up from my stomach to the milk source and latched on. My baby was learning to trust at my breast, and I was learning to trust my body, my Creator and the people who stick around when it's messy. I think of Jesus telling Nicodemus, "You must be born again."[114] We become reborn when we learn to trust, and trust is hard labor. God has given us mothers and fathers in the faith to help us in the delivery.[115] He has made us to cling, even as grownups,[116] because he trusts that our relationships will lead us to his love.[117]

Father trust

> Father, little children must grow up. And to grow we've got to learn to trust. And to trust we've got to cling to You.[118]

Adolescents want love but fear the exposure and possible rejection. They try to be loved without being known. They are afraid to ask and afraid to trust.

Children are willing to receive and be cared for. They ask for things and expect to get them. They clamor for attention. A childlike relationship with Jesus is the way into the kingdom. But we can't stop at becoming children. We have to become infants.

---

112 Luke 8:1-3
113 Psalm 22:9
114 John 3:7
115 Isaiah 49:15, 66:13
116 Genesis 2:24; Matthew 19:4-6; Ephesians 5:31-32; Proverbs 18:24
117 John 15:12-13, 17:24-26; Ephesians 4:15-16
118 Meece, David. "Learning to Trust." *Learning to Trust.* Star Song Records, 1992, CD

Babies want their mommies. That's it. The mommy is the source of food, comfort, warmth, companionship. The mommy protects and nurtures and nourishes. The mommy takes care of everything and is everything.

I think of the classic children's book[119] about the mother bird who is out looking for worms when her baby hatches. Her baby enters the world alone and starts trying to find its mother. Maybe it's a book about co-dependence: I can't find my mother, and I need one. So, how about I make *you* my mother?

I remember talking to God about my fears in relationship. The conversation itself was evidence of my growing up into a kid. I used to not trust God enough to ask him questions. A friend of mine was getting busier, and I didn't know what that meant for me or for our friendship. I asked God, "Is my friend no longer available to me? Does she not want to be with me anymore? Should I let her go?" Maybe these are legitimate questions. But they were causing me more anxiety than grief. There is sadness in contemplating loss, but why was I afraid? God answered me, not in audible words, but with an understanding that should have taken hours to explain but only took about five seconds. This is how I understood His answer:

> When you chose her as a friend, you were also subconsciously choosing her to make up for what your parents didn't give you. She has chosen you as a friend, but she has not chosen these expectations you have put on her. And she cannot fulfill them. She can be your friend without all that weight. You can simply enjoy her for who she is and who she is becoming. Let *me* fulfill your expectations. Let *me* be that parent and love away that fear. I am available. Every minute. Every day. For the rest of your (eternal) life.

He had said this to me before when I was out "looking for my mother," but I believed him this time. I felt the weight and the fear fall off. I invited him to heal the deep wounds, and he settled me with his love!

> The god of this world has blinded the minds of the unbelievers, to keep them from seeing the light of the gospel of the glory of Christ, who is the image of God... For God, who said, "Let light shine out of darkness," has shone in our hearts to give the light of the knowledge of the glory of God in the face of Jesus Christ. [120]

119 Eastman, P.D. *Are You My Mother?* Random House, 1960
120 2 Corinthians 4:4,6

Infancy is looking up into the face of God: "Oh, *you're* my mother."

David said, "Delight yourself in the LORD, and he will give you the desires of your heart."[121] It is childlike to look to the Lord to give us what we want. We come close to him, expecting a blessing. And time with him changes us into babies. He *becomes* the blessing, and delighting in him becomes the one desire of our hearts.

The prodigal son was childlike in his asking for a premature inheritance. His father gave him what he wanted and the space to realize that he didn't really want it after all. The boy spent all he had coming to him and eventually came home to his real inheritance. He left as a child and came home as a baby. His older brother was stuck in adolescence.[122]

We leave father and mother to be united to Christ and the church, but sometimes we find the church before we find Christ. We find Jesus' mother and brothers and like them so much that we decide to make them all that we need. This is co-dependence. We need *Jesus*. We need to be born again as babies, dependent on and delighting in God our Father. Spiritual adolescents are looking to be OK on their own. Children are looking for good gifts to help them through. Babies live in total dependence of the light of the knowledge of the glory of God in the face of Jesus Christ.

A mother and her sons

> You, therefore, have no excuse, you who pass judgment on someone else, For at whatever point you judge another, you are condemning yourself, because you who pass judgment do the same things. Now we know that God's judgment against those who do such things is based on truth. So, when you, a mere human being, pass judgment on them and yet do the same things, do you think you will escape God's judgment? Or do you show contempt for the riches of his kindness, forbearance and patience, not realizing that God's kindness is intended to lead you to repentance?[123]

Here's a story about a mother and her sons trying to find their way. The oldest son at age ten was at his grandma's house and in need of a shower, but he had forgotten his clean clothes in the car. "He said he didn't want to get them and asked instead if his mother would bring them to him. When she refused, he asked if he could just put the clothes he was wearing back on. She said no. Neither would back down, and the boy

121 Psalm 37:4
122 Luke 15:11-32
123 Romans 2:1-4, New International Version

was revving up, so his mother sent him upstairs for five minutes. Afterwards, he still refused to get his clothes and started to argue again. The mother talked to her husband about it. He said a whack with a spatula will snap him out of rebellion. The mother didn't like hitting her children, because she usually did it impulsively, when she was angry at them. She thought, *I don't hit other people, so why should I hit my children?* The husband found a spatula and went to find his son. There was more arguing but no whacking. The son got his clothes out of the car and came back into the house still arguing. The mother felt attacked and disrespected. She felt like he shouldn't talk to her that way and get away with it. So, she went to find the spatula and take care of business herself. She attempted to whack her son on the leg with the spatula, but he blocked her. She waited till he moved his hands. He said he wouldn't argue anymore, just don't hit him. She took aim and smacked him on the leg. The spatula broke. This added fuel to the son's fire: "You broke the spatula on me!" He had no remorse, only indignation. So, his mother took a shower brush, whacked him on the arm and left him crying in the bathroom.

The mother hadn't lost her temper, but she had broken her own rules. She felt muddy and angry and guilty inside. The son cried and cried, and the mother wanted to know what tragic story he was telling himself to be so sad. He had locked himself in the bathroom, but he let his mother in when she asked. He was still sitting on the floor with his clothes on, sobbing in his arms over the toilet seat. "Why are you still crying?" she asked. "Why are you so sad?"

"We used to solve our problems peacefully. I don't like violence."

"We have always argued. And I have spanked you in the past. I don't remember solving our problems peacefully."

He said, "We would fight, and then you would say you were sorry, and I would say I was sorry, and we would have peace again."

"I would say I was sorry for losing my temper and saying mean things and hitting you when I was angry. I didn't do that this time. I was punishing you for your disrespect."

"Oh, you weren't angry? You hit me and you weren't angry?! That's even worse! When you hit me, it makes me hate you. It makes me want to hit you back."

The son was crying in the bathroom, hating his mother and wanting to hit her. And still not taking his shower. It was obviously a power struggle. And aren't parents supposed to win those? Spare the spatula, spoil the child? The mother felt defeated. Her son preferred fights where he provoked her and she sinned in her anger and had to apologize. He wanted to win as much as she did, and her sinning felt like winning to him. Obeying her felt like losing.

The spatula and shower brush had accomplished nothing good. The mother went back to the bathroom door and told the boy he had five minutes to get in the shower or he would not get to stay the night with his cousins as was planned. The crying stopped and the sound of water started almost immediately. He didn't want to obey her, but he also didn't want to miss out on something that he wanted to do.

The boy is now eleven and a raging, unpredictable sea. His mother has tried at turns to contain him, diagnose him, change him, pacify him, ignore him, shame him and punish him. Because she is afraid of being in the storm with him. When she gets close to him, he exposes her. He rages and mourns the imperfections in himself and others, and it exposes her own raging and mourning heart. He accuses her of things that are not her fault, and it exposes the little girl in her, confused at her own father's accusations. It makes her feel crazy. It makes her want to run. But this boy is not her father. He is her son. And he needs her to love him. Right where he is.

It feels wrong to submit to her children. She put in her time being bullied, and now it's her turn to bully. It's her turn to be right. To make the rules. To say what she wants. To do what she wants. It's her turn to take the sins of the fathers out on the sons.

It feels wrong to submit to *anyone*. As wrong as death.

This mother's boys were fighting before school. She asked them twice to stop. The third time she said they would lose their ten-minute online game playing for the day. The younger said nothing. The older started arguing. "Why do you care if we fight? We always fight. You don't have to get involved. It's my brother's fault. He was going to throw his shoe at my kitten. I had to do something. Can we have our tablet time back?" She said no.

"I hate how you're always threatening us! You just want power. You're not thinking about us. We don't care if we fight. You want peace, so you make us stop. Why don't you just leave us alone and let us fight?"

They headed to school, and the older son kept complaining and accusing. His mother had become his enemy, because she was not giving him what he wanted. She told him he was making things worse for himself and it would be better if he would shut up. He said, "My life would be better if *you* shut up. God doesn't punish this way. God lets you go until the end and then he decides. My teacher doesn't treat me this way. She cares about me. She doesn't punish me. You don't care about me. You only care about it being peaceful. You only care about yourself."

The mother drove away with rocks in her ribcage. She wanted to run away. Since she couldn't, she started thinking of places she could send her older boy for the summer. She wanted to be done with this relationship. It was causing her too much pain. When she got home, she wrote him a letter.

> You have said some hard things to me, these last days. I know you said them when you were angry at not getting what you want, but still, you said them. And words have power. Words have meaning. Even though I care about you and love you and am trying hard to be a good parent, you are saying that you do not believe this is true. So, I want to take you seriously and stop trying to have a relationship with you. Because relationship is about talking and listening to one another. And you do not seem to want that right now. And honestly, the way you treat me and speak to me, I don't really want it either right now.
>
> I was thinking about what you asked about how God interacts with people. Basically, if a person doesn't want to believe God and worship God, then God leaves that person alone and lets them pursue evil. God withdraws from relationship. And THAT is punishment enough. Living outside of relationship with God is...hell. But God is patient and merciful. He is the father who is always waiting for us to come back to him, and when we do, he will celebrate us.
>
> Anyway, we still live together, so there will be interactions, and there are house rules that everyone has to abide by and house chores that need to get done so that things run smoothly. And it's for everyone's good to do these things. You use the resources, so you are responsible to help keep things running and orderly. You do not want to be treated like a kid, and yet you do. Because kids do a lot less work than adults. At least in our house. You are barely responsible for anything. You seem to want to do nothing and have others still feed you and entertain you and buy you things. You are getting too old for that kind of irresponsibility.
>
> I am praying for you. That you really do find what you want. I believe that we all really want Jesus. That we want to be slaves to righteousness more than slaves to sin (John 8:34; Romans 6:16). But it is a battle. To

play by the rules of love. Jesus calls it losing our lives to find them. I hope in this time of struggling and searching that you turn to the Bible and conversation with God for answers.

I love you.

When the son came home from school and read the letter, he was furious. At himself most of all. Because he wanted relationship with his mother more than the thing he was fighting for, and now he had lost both. He could see no way back to goodness. He started growling and hitting himself in the head. Then he banged his head against the refrigerator. His mother told him to go outside and not damage the appliances. He asked if he could bang his head on the concrete. His mother said it would not be wise, but she couldn't stop him. She paced and prayed for her son's protection. She looked out the window and saw him weeping in a patch of mint.

He came back in the house, face flushed and eyes wild.

"Can you just kill me?" he asked.

"No, I won't kill you."

"I don't like myself. I don't like my life." He threw himself onto a chair and cried some more.

"Just tell God you're sorry. Just ask Him for help, and He will help you," his mother said.

"It's too late for that," the boy said. "It's too late for me."

"That's a lie! The devil is stealing the truth from you."

"Well, he must need it."

"Resist the devil and come near to God," the mother urged. And then she left him to make dinner. She could not choose for him.

Her younger son had soccer practice at 5:30. Her husband said he would be home before she had to take him. At 5:40, he still wasn't. She told her son to call him, because she felt a storm brewing in her head that would come out of her mouth if she opened it. He'd be home in ten minutes. She waited in the car, hoping the metal around her would contain the storm. That's when she realized that she and her firstborn were caught in the same storm. When people let her down, they became her enemies. And she turned on them, even if she loved them. Even if they loved her. She couldn't do this anymore. It was her turn to die to the sins of the fathers, mothers, husbands and sons. It was her turn to leave them at the foot of the cross.

That night, before bed, the older son was crying again. He said to his mother, "I don't want to be alone. I want to be with you. I want it to be like it used to be, when you would snuggle with me and talk to me. We have been fighting for days. I want a reset."

"I know. But not tonight. I need a break. I'm tired, and I'm going to bed."

"Why don't you even care? I cried at school today about us fighting. I feel so bad and you are just standing there. You are so serious. You don't even feel bad."

"I *do* feel bad. And I *do* care. But you have hurt me with your words. I don't want to get close to you right now. I don't want to show you how I feel."

"But all I want is to be close to you."

"But you're so mean to me. No one is as mean to me as you."

"I know. I don't know why I say the things I say. I don't mean them. And I *did* ask God for help today."

The mother kissed her older boy goodnight and left him to kiss the younger and get ready for bed. They met again in the bathroom, where he was brushing his teeth through his tears. "I'm sorry." he said. "You were right to punish me. You did nothing wrong. I'm sorry for what I said to you and how I behaved. It took me all day to realize it, but I know now that I was wrong."

"I forgive you," the mother said. She put her hand on her son's heart. "You are clean. That is your reset."

She saw the tension leave her boy's face and peace replace the tears in his eyes. Tomorrow, another storm might threaten, but today love had won.

Loving Fearlessly

Tracks heading toward the Ambassador Bridge and the Renaissance Center, Detroit 2003

Constant Contact

As the Father has loved me, so have I loved you. Abide in my love.[124]

And pray in the Spirit on all occasions with all kinds of prayers and requests. With this in mind, be alert and always keep on praying for all the Lord's people.[125]

Constant Contact® is the name of an online marketing company that helps businesses stay in the minds of potential customers through a steady stream of emails. The idea is that people will want whatever is being advertised as long as they are frequently reminded that they do. Facebook, too, is a form of personal online marketing: *you will want me if I just keep sending you my best pictures and wittiest thoughts.* The modern mode of relationship is constant, fear-based contact. My husband told me about a German article written over a decade ago, in which the writer compares 21st century social interactions to the flight patterns (murmuration) of birds. A flock of starlings can change directions at a moment's notice. Although it is unclear who is leading or what direction the flock will head in next, all the birds move in it together. The writer compares this to young people trying to decide on a Friday night destination. Although they may start in one direction, like going to a party at someone's house, in the course of communicating back and forth, they may suddenly shift directions completely, so that no one goes to the party and everyone ends up at a nightclub on the other side of town. Or someone might ask a few friends over. Then those friends talk to other friends, and, depending on where the flock is headed, those few friends may never show up or they may bring fifty others with them. The only way to stay current on where the friend flock is headed is constant contact.

Even with the constant contact of lightning speed internet, five million Facebook friends, Snapchat, Instagram, Twitter and unlimited phone service, we will never feel connected enough. It is trust that truly connects us. Contact without trust means constant vigilance and striving for a taste of eternity that constantly eludes us. We were meant for constant contact with the living God. We can trust the Father and his gifts for us. He does not change like shifting shadows[126] or a flock of birds. We were meant to abide in his love. We have constant access to his love and attention. If we can rescue our attention from all the other sources trying to contact us, we will find him. If we turn our attention toward him, there he is.

---

124 John 15:9
125 Ephesians 6:18
126 James 1:17

Sometimes, I am restless for affection, hoping for a word of encouragement or acknowledgment, straining for a sign that I am not alone and that my existence matters to someone. I'm fighting to stay connected, trying to keep up with the flock and losing myself in the process. Then I remember Jesus' words to me: *As the Father has loved me, so have I loved you. Abide in my love.* His love is mine. Constantly. I just have to remain in it. I can confess my fear and unbelief and ask him for the fullness of his presence. He fills me till I overflow with praise and adoration, as love wins in my heart.

Trust is a constant conversation with the invisible One. The Holy Spirit connects us to the Father and to one another, in the deepest of ways. But we have to trust him enough to let go of the flock and stop looking for eternity in externals.

More than enough

I struggle with healthy boundaries of enoughness. I grew up with a "less than" complex and have been trying to compensate ever since.

My daughter, Elli, slept well on her own at four months. At five months, she started waking more and wanting more. She'd sleep a few hours and then cry for me. I'd feed her to sleep and put her back in her crib, and she'd cry again. If I picked her up, she'd stop. I began sleeping with her in Jaben's bottom bunk, just to get more sleep. One early morning, I knew things had to change. We were both up and irritable. Instead of being grateful for my night efforts, she just wanted more. I felt used. I liked being close to her and feeling needed and wanted, but I didn't like feeling as if she owned me. Was love winning in the night? Or fear? Love always trusts, and I wasn't trusting her to be ok in the night without me. I wasn't trusting her ability to fall asleep on her own. I was giving in to all of her demands and starting to feel resentful.

What does love look like when one person wants more than the other person can freely give?

When I am on the shores of a lake or ocean, I can get overwhelmed by the beauty and goodness I experience there. My desire to capture it and never leave it can cause me to mentally leave prematurely. I get distracted from really *being* there by my fear of *leaving* there. I decide to look for a rock or a shell to take with me as consolation or remembrance. It's like, I start feeling out of control about leaving, so I look for something to hold on to. I usually find some good rocks or shells, but what if there are better ones that I am *not* finding? I start obsessing and feel out of control again, as I scour the sand for the elusive best find. I'm filling my hands and my pockets, but

I'm still looking. What am I looking for? What am I trying to secure? Even if I find an agate or a moon shell, is it really mine to take? Why can't I just leave the beauty and goodness as I found it, trusting it will be there for me when I return?

At a time when I was feeling that Christoph and I were missing the beauty and goodness of each other, he suggested that we take half an hour each evening to listen to each other. One night, it would be my turn to talk and he would listen, asking questions if he had any. The next night, he would talk and I would listen. It sounded amazing. Too good to be true. I was skeptical about it lasting. I was afraid to get my hopes up and let my guard down, only to be disappointed and abandoned. "'Yes," I said. "Let's do it. But *you* have to initiate." Christoph said that he would. The first night, I asked him to talk first. So, he did. We poured ourselves some red wine and sat by the wood burning stove. He told me about what was going on at work, which made sense, since he spent most of his time there. However, I was feeling at a disadvantage, since the things I would talk about would probably make me cry, and I was already worried about this space being safe. The next evening, I watched and waited to see what would happen. After dinner, Christoph pulled some chairs together near the stove and sat down. I sat down next to him. He took my hand and looked into my eyes. "What do you want to tell me?" he asked. I think I started crying right then. It was so sweet by the fire, having Christoph near and attentive to my heart. When he left to put the boys to bed, I sat there and cried some more — because of the sweetness, the rawness, and my fear of it ending.

We never did it again. Christoph didn't initiate the next night, and I didn't either (although I was watching and waiting). And it disappeared from our lives as suddenly as it had entered. At the time, I saw it as proof that he wasn't committed to knowing me and being known. I saw it as failure and neglect. But I have been married to Christoph over twenty years now, and he has never wavered in his commitment to me. I know that he is a safe place for me to come to, even when there's no wood-burning stove, no red wine, and no scheduled time for the two of us. We have three kids now—two pre-adolescents and one baby. These days, if we would try to get that half hour of listening in after dinner each night, it would not be the ocean of beauty and goodness that I'm longing for. We are often occupied with other needs and obligations, but our hearts are toward each other. And sometimes we find each other, unexpectedly, at the dinner table or in the yard or on a walk or in the car. We enter into the deep beauty and goodness of knowing each other and loving each other. Sometimes, we get everyone in bed by 9, including ourselves, and laugh and talk and cry and pray and stay close to each other for a while. And sometimes we don't.

It would be easier for me to trust if I didn't have to.

I used to stare at Christoph while he slept, trying to hoard his nearness so I would have enough when he left for work. I guess that is why I struggle to let Elli cry at night, when I could just hold her close and she would stop. I share with her the ache for nearness. I fight to hold beauty and goodness close. But it's never enough. Kate and I had a hoarding phase in our friendship. We could spend a whole day together, and, the next day, I'd want to do it all over again. For a while, we had this four-hour-a-week limit of togetherness, so we didn't hang out all the time. And four hours seems ample, right? But what if our kids had soccer together or we were at a baby shower or birthday party together? Could we add that to our time?

I could just keep filling my heart with beauty and goodness and never have enough.

God has set eternity in our hearts.[127] And I believe this is why we are voracious for eternal things. We want unending beauty and goodness. We want love without fear. We want safety and belonging. And we *have* them. In our hearts. We have God's Spirit, guaranteeing our inheritance.[128] But it is easier to trust this is true, when we don't have to. So, we keep reaching for some form of external assurance that we are safe and loved and close to beauty. At least *I* do. And sometimes, I actually touch it. I feel it. I feel safe and loved and enveloped in beauty. And I cling to those moments. But they are not meant to last. And they are not mine to cling to. Because I am actually clinging to a person, an experience, a place, an unchangeability that does not yet exist. Within hours or minutes, circumstances change, and I grow fearful again. I start reaching again for eternity. It's a way of trying to save my life, but I'm actually losing it. It's making a person or a place or a feeling my paradise away from paradise. It's like Jesus' friends being sure at the Passover meal that they were in the right place with the right guy. But then the beautiful time together was over. It was dark outside. Jesus was crossing the brook of sorrow and entering the garden of surrender. And suddenly, they were very, very tired and afraid.

The way into the garden of eternity is through the garden of Gethsemane. *Not my will, but yours, God.* This is the place of beauty and belonging — the place of trusting, because we *have* to. And in this place, he ministers to us and assures our hearts that his ever-present love for us is more than enough.

127 Ecclesiastes 3:11
128 Ephesians 1:14

Walking the walk

> Whoever says he abides in [Jesus Christ] ought to walk in the same way in which he walked.[129]

Jesus came for the outcasts of Eden. He came with eternity in his heart. He came to lead us back into perfect relationship with him. *Forever.* This is the joy that motivated him to endure the cross.[130] He came to a people who had never walked with God in the cool of the day.[131] So, Jesus had to convince them that walking with him was walking back to God. How was he going to do this? What was his strategy?

Surrender.[132]

First, in baptism, where the Spirit descended upon him and the Father spoke his love and pleasure. Then to the Spirit's leading. Into the wilderness to face the devil. The Spirit was with Jesus in the emptiness and temptation. This was not abandonment; this was deep relationship. In those forty days, Jesus was hearing the voice of God and being sustained by His Words. He was giving himself completely to the Spirit's love and leadership. He was worshiping.[133] When the devil came to play on his fears, there weren't any fears to play on. Jesus believed that the Words of God would sustain him. He did not need to conjure up other sources of nourishment. He did not need to test or prove God's care for him. He was living in it. Depending on it.

Dependence is worship.

Jesus came out of the wilderness with an invitation: "Repent, for the kingdom of heaven has come near!"[134] I think it was like saying, *you can walk with God again, if you walk with me.* He called to Peter and Andrew, whom he saw fishing, "Come follow me, and I will make you fishers of men."[135] It was an invitation into surrender and transcendence: *Trust me more than you trust yourself, and we'll do more than catch fish together. We'll change eternity!*

He's saying it to us, too. Right now. I am sure of it. Maybe you currently have no deep relationships. Or maybe your relationships are so deep you're drowning in them. In both cases, you have misplaced your worship. You can find it again in the

---

129 I John 2:6
130 Hebrews 12:2
131 Genesis 3:8
132 Philippians 2:6-8
133 Romans 12:1
134 Matthew 4:17, New International Version
135 Matthew 4:19

garden: *Not my will, but yours, God.* His will is to lead us to the green pastures and still waters of his love and care. His will is to give us good gifts and good traveling companions. His will is that love wins in our lives. If love is not winning in your life, then you are not living from the Words of his mouth. I encourage you to walk away from whatever has its hooks in you and come to the waters of repentance. Let the Spirit wash over you and the fire of forgiveness burn away all fears of punishment.[136] The Spirit will lead you back to God, each minute of each day, as you stay in constant contact.

Breaking the silence

> There is no fear in love, but perfect love casts out fear. For fear has to do with punishment, and whoever fears has not been perfected in love.[137]

When I was in first grade, I took Hope Grant's eraser. While Hope read from the Puggs reading book, her eraser rolled off her lap and under my chair. Very slowly, very smoothly, I picked it up and slipped it into my pocket. I thought she saw me, but she didn't. I was hoping she would miss it, because I didn't want her old eraser anyway. As we were pushing our chairs back to our desks, I noticed Hope searching around her chair. I grinned victoriously. I was just about to return the eraser when Hope ran to the teacher and said, "Someone took my eraser. I had it in reading group, and now I can't find it."

To my horror, Ms. Clendinen announced, "Class, Hope is missing an eraser. Has anyone seen it?" No one had. My heart began to ache, and my throat got lumpy. I couldn't give Hope her eraser *now.* The whole class would know I had taken it. I kept it in my pocket and carried it home.

In silence, I hurried to my bedroom and shut the door. I took the eraser out of my pocket and stared at it. It was green and dirty with holes gouged out by pencil lead. I went into my closet and closed the door behind me. With head pounding and heart racing, I set the green eraser at the bottom of my box of play clothes. I left it there, but the guilt stayed with me. I couldn't get away from it. I thought it might help if I threw the eraser away. A few days later, I retrieved the dirty eraser and took it outside to the big trash can in the garage, so no one would find it and ask questions. When I came out of the garage, I saw my mom standing on the front porch.

"What are you doing?" she asked.

---

136 Mathew 3:11; I John 4:18
137 I John 4:18

"Just throwing something away," I said. She looked puzzled but said nothing else.

One year later, when my mom picked me up from school, I told her about the eraser. "Why are you telling me this *now*?" she asked. It was because that morning in chapel, Dr. Rhodes had talked about confessing sins, and the green eraser burned in my heart again. I wanted to be free of it, once and for all. I was afraid of how my mom might respond, but I couldn't keep it to myself any longer. The guilt had grown too big in me. So, I told her. Like a balloon being pulled at the mouth and screeching out its air, confession is a grating exhale. Afterwards, though, shame is deflated.

Jesus made this possible. He canceled the record of debt.[138]

> He was pierced for our transgressions; he was crushed for our iniquities; upon him was the chastisement that brought us peace, and with his wounds we are healed.[139]

There are dirtier secrets than a dirty eraser, but Jesus bore the punishment of them all. He disarmed the demonic powers by not being ashamed to die for sins that were not even his own. His perfect love neutralizes fear and reverses shame.[140] We know we are abiding in this love [141] when we find ourselves breaking the awkward silences with confession and forgiveness. In college, I reached out to people I didn't know with the message of a loving Jesus that I didn't know. Decades later, I am letting Jesus reach in to me with his love, and it's letting me know him and freeing me to be known by him without fear. I screw up all the time — more than ever, it seems. But I don't have to be fearful about it. Jesus loves me. He took on humanness and death so I could be fearless in my humanness and fearless in my love for him and others.

Shame that is rooted in fear wants to hide. If I fear I am only loved when I deserve it, then I won't want to disclose anything that would make me seem less deserving. If I say something unkind, forget to do what I said I would do, screw up a task, steal an eraser, I don't want to give anyone more reason to not love me. So, I keep these things hidden as much as possible. When I can't hide them, I blame other people. But this only arms the dark powers and further isolates me from love. God sees us and knows us anyway. There is nothing hidden from him.[142] As I come to know and believe in the love he has for me,[143] I become bolder in breaking shameful silences.

---

138 Colossians 2:15, Philippians 2:8
139 Isaiah 53:5
140 Romans 5:20
141 John 15:9
142 Hebrews 4:13
143 I John 4:16

I'm sorry.

I forgive you.

These are silence breaking words that disarm demons. These are powerful choices to love more than fear.

I can let go of vengeance, pride, and self-preservation when I am clinging to God's love for me as my safe place. I can be stripped of every external thing I have because of the garden within, which is my secret abundance of care and decadent love. The Kingdom of God is within me. It is kept safe there. Nothing can separate me from the love of God.

Is forgiveness legitimate, or even possible, if the other person isn't sorry or hasn't admitted guilt? I think of Jesus on the cross, saying, *Father, forgive them, for they know not what they do.*[144] This was Jesus loving his enemies. This was Jesus dying for us before it even mattered to us. The forgiving kept Jesus connected to God's love and made it possible for us to be connected, too. I think it is similar for us. We forgive to stay connected to the love and forgiveness of God.[145] We also give others the opportunity to connect to us and God as well, but they may not choose to.

I really like the Four-Way Forgiveness Prayer described in the book, *Released to Soar.*[146] It is a prayer to pray in the presence of others who are safe, though it can also be used when alone. The first step is to describe the offender's acts that hurt you and the ways they made you feel and to symbolically take them in one hand and place them in the other. Then you lift these acts and feelings to Jesus. You, or the person praying with you, ask Jesus to take the hurt from these offenses and heal and redeem. The second step is to confess any ways that the hurt done to you has caused you to hurt others. You take the hurts you've caused in one hand and place them in the other, as you name them. Then you empty your hands at the foot of the cross, letting Jesus forgive you and forget them. The third and fourth steps are prayers of blessing, first for the offender and then for yourself. How do you want God to bless the offender? What blessings from God do you want for yourself? I have joined others in their forgiveness prayers and experienced how praying them has unburdened them and freed them to love without fear. For myself, I have come to realize that, when I wake up in the morning and don't want to face myself or others... when I want to run away, leave town and/or escape from my life, it means that I am in need of forgiving and forgiveness. If, instead of running, I hold out to God the hurts I've suffered and

---

144 Luke 23:34
145 Matthew 6:12,15
146 Boelens, Peter and Evelyn. *Released to Soar.* The Write Place, 2010

the hurts I've caused, my defenses crumble and my tears overflow. Somewhere in the blessing and being blessed, I've entered the garden. *Not my will, but yours, God.* His Spirit ministers to me. My tears of sorrow turn to tears of joy. The cross has been endured. Shame has been scorned. I am clean. I belong. I can love again.

Becoming Bread

Truly, truly, I say to you, unless a grain of wheat falls into the earth and dies, it remains alone; but if it dies, it bears much fruit.[147]

Entering the garden means accepting the will of the Father that we, too, become provision for the world, through our death. As we die to our fears, we become alive to Christ and food for the world. When Jesus lived on earth, he was baptized and led by the Spirit into the wilderness. He came out preaching repentance, performing miracles and loving fearlessly to the death. As we abide in Jesus and walk as he walked, the Spirit leads us to the wilderness, too. In the wilderness, the Spirit teaches us who God is and who the devil is. We are softened by God's gentleness, healed by his humility, and sustained by his words. We learn to resist the devil and come near to God. We learn that God's love and power are enough for us. As the Spirit leads us out of the wilderness and into impossible situations, we trust that God's supernatural provision is enough to be broken and shared. When others have needs, we rely on God in us to meet those needs. As we are nourished by God's love and strength, we can nourish others. As we steal away to the garden and other solitary places,[148] the Spirit teaches us about *becoming* the provision.

At the last supper before His crucifixion, Jesus took bread, gave thanks and broke it, saying, "This is my body, which is given for you. Do this in remembrance of me."[149] We remember what he did for us by breaking bread. We also remember who he is and who we are by *being* bread, broken and shared. We invite strangers home for dinner. We turn our cheeks to hostility. We grieve when our hearts are broken. We forgive and bless. We love fearlessly, because God has loved the fear out of us. We show up where it's messy, as a seed planted in the soil of relationship. We die to our selfishness, right in the middle of weeds, and grow into something delicious. Others taste and see that the Lord we are surrendered to is good, and it changes them. Weeds turn into wheat in an instant of believing.

147 John 12:24
148 Mark 1:35; Luke 5:16
149 Luke 22:19

Epilogue

Everything Else

One of my favorite books is *Grover and the Everything in the Whole Wide World Museum.*[150] Grover visits the *Small Hall*, the *Tall Hall*, the *Long Thin Things You Can Write with Room*, the *Carrot Room*, the *Things That Make So Much Noise You Can't Hear Yourself Think Room* and many others. As Grover is nearing the end of the museum, he muses to himself that he has seen a lot but he hasn't seen everything in the whole wide world yet. But when he sees some double doors with a sign over them that says, *Everything Else,* he says, "*Aha!*" And walks through the exit doors into the whole wide world.

This, too, is a point of exit and entrance. I have written about what I have learned and seen, but I have only shared a few rooms in the whole wide world of relationships. In the wilderness of our minds and hearts, Satan comes with all kinds of crazy propositions, but it all comes down to love winning over fear. God loves us, and Satan lies to us. We choose love or lies. We know we are listening to lies when we are afraid. We know we are listening to love when we are not.

I leave you with this benediction, loved fearless ones. God said it to me at a time when I was feeling the pressure of the garden life. And if you've read this far, I believe God must be saying it to you, too.

> I'm taking you deeper into love, so you can go deeper into the valleys with my hurting ones. I will go with you. My arm around you is my love yoke, my pleasure in you, my strength for you. In this world you will have trouble, but take heart hold onto your heart, fill it to bursting with my love and my good pleasure and the HOPE of my kingdom coming in and through you — for I have overcome the world. And to you who overcomes, I will give the right to sit with me on my throne, just as I overcame and sat down with my Father on his throne.

Hallelujah. What a Savior!

---

150 Stiles, Norman and Daniel Wilcox. *Grover and the Everything in the Whole Wide World Museum.* Random House Books for Young Readers, 1974

Shares & Prayers

Trust is an ongoing conversation. Just reading about trust won't grow it. The following questions are meant to be answered in conversation with God and others who want to know you and love you. You can, of course, discuss the chapters together and come up with your own questions for each other. The guidelines are simply to keep your times together personal, honest (Ephesians 4:15-16), confidential (James 4:11), worshipful (Romans 12:1-2) and encouraging (I Thessalonians 5:11; Hebrews 10:24).

Introduction

Share: Jesus' decisions led him to the Garden of Gethsemane. Where have your decisions led you? What do you not want to live without?

Prayer: Have the rich ruler conversation with Jesus. (Matt. 19:16-30; Mark 10:17-31; Luke 18:18-30)

> "Jesus, I have tried to please you by..."
> "Is this what you want from me? What do you want from me?"

Exploding Dreams

Being human is a dream deferred

Share: What are some dreams you've had for your life?

Prayer: Ask Jesus what he's dreaming about you and what dreams he wants to come true in your life.

The heart of God

Share: Think about whom you trust and whom you don't. What does a relationship based on trust look like?

Prayer: Ask Jesus to expose and explode whatever gets in the way of trusting him.

Passion without trust

Share: Do you love anyone or anything as much as or more than Jesus? Is this the thing or person you have to be without in order to follow him?

Prayer: Ask Jesus to expose any idols in your life.

An ongoing conversation

Share: Were there situations this past week where your response to someone was motivated more by fear than by love?

Prayer: Sit at Jesus' feet and invite him to expose your fears (lies) and then love them away (with truth).

Pause is the real play

Share: If you could be on Sabbatical right now and just spend your days doing things and being with people who refresh you, what would a Sabbatical week look like for you?

Prayer: Ask Jesus what he wants you to throw off to make your everyday look more like the Sabbatical you are dreaming of.

Gold in clay houses

Share: Where do you best meet God and how do you best connect with God? (On your own? With others? In nature? In the morning? While walking? In little bits or in a longer getaway?)

Prayer: Ask him how and where you can practically make more space for the treasure of him.

Dreaming God's dreams

Share: What acts of service or religious commitments are getting in the way of God's dreams for you?

Prayer: Ask Jesus what he wants you to do about it.

Enemies

Catching Foxes

Share: In the battlefield of your mind, what negative thoughts do you most easily believe and get discouraged by?

Prayer: Take time catching those foxes together and replacing lies with truth.

Offensive Jesus

Share: Has Jesus ever offended you by not responding the way you expected him to?

Prayer: Bring those offenses to Jesus and listen for his response.

Exposure to love

Share: How do you handle disappointment? Think of a time this past week that you were disappointed. What did you think and say and do about it?

Prayer: Share those disappointments with Jesus and let him lead you into redemption of the situation and the relationship.

Bread, care and power

Share: Talk about your own temptations to get what you want and provide for yourself without waiting on God or others.

Prayer: Take some time to open your hands and your heart and give God what you are holding on to, in exchange for what he wants to give you.

> "God, I give you my fear of/tendency to/hoarding of/control over..."

> "Please bless me with your abundance of..."

The defeated enemy

Share: Which of these three interactions Jesus had (with the wild-looking man, the woman with a past, the friend with control issues) speaks to you personally? In what way?

Prayer: Spend some time praying for each other, that Jesus would draw you to himself (John 12:32) and fill you with (more) Spirit power to be active witnesses (Acts 1:8) of the defeated enemy and the conquering King!

What does love look like?

Share: Whom in your life do you currently struggle to love well? [Note: do not use this time to slander another. It may be wisest to just answer the first question in your head and share answers to the second question] What is your natural response when offended or hurt?

Prayer: Tell Jesus about these hard relationships and ask him to reveal what it would look like for you to love these people well.

In the presence of my enemies

Share: Have you experienced things that have brought God's goodness and care for you into question?

Prayer: Be still and ask God to show you where he was in those experiences.

The winter is past

Share: Are there memories, hurts, fears you're holding onto that are freezing your heart and killing the life trying to grow there?

Prayer: Listen and respond as Jesus says to you, *'Arise my love, my beautiful one, and come away' from death and despair and barrenness and loneliness. Our love can bloom. We can sing. We can have beauty. We can have growth. Come away.*

Body Reality

Church

Share: Talk about a relationship or an experience with someone that has grown your trust.

Prayer: Listen together for what Jesus is saying about letting more love into your heart.

Known and loved

Share: Describe yourself as a teenager. Are there parts of you still stuck there?

Prayer: Give those parts to Jesus and remind each other in prayer that you belong to God and are accepted and wanted and deeply loved.

Learning to trust

Share: Are there people or circumstances you try to control? Are there people or circumstances controlling you?

Prayer: Entrust God with these fears and control moves.

One Flesh

Share: What do you think it means to be nourished and cherished by Christ? What would it look like for you (the church) to nourish and cherish each other?

Prayer: Ask God to show you personal and practical ways to increase love and unity in the body.

Coming close to Jesus

Share: What would it look like for you to come close to Jesus? What fears cause you to keep your distance?

Prayer: Get a partner and take turns being at Jesus feet in worship and repentance and speaking Jesus' words to each other: "Your sins are forgiven. Your faith has healed you. Go in peace."

Coming close to one another.

Share: Who is it hard for you to serve? To be served by?

Prayer: Wash each other's feet. If not literally, then demonstrate this with some other act of service or prayer of blessing. Take turns being Jesus to one another.

Parents and Children

Growing up into a kid

Share: Whose voices do you listen to and whose expectations do you try to fulfill?

Prayer: Speak God's expectations over one another. (faith, coming close, confession, forgiveness...)

Leaving home and saying goodbye

Share: Talk about your relationship with your parents. Where are you in the leaving home process?

Prayer: Take turns giving your unfulfilled childhood expectations (what you expected of your parents and/or what they expected of you that went unfulfilled) to God in prayer.

Re-Parenting

Share: Who is parenting you these days? Whom do you listen to and fear disappointing?

Prayer: Seek God on what it looks like to really trust him and one another, and pray for that trust to grow!

Father trust

Share: Have you ever been looking for your mother or father in other people? Or looking for your own mother or father to be God?

Prayer: Spend time meditating on the way God the Father parents us and pray about being that kind of parent to one another. (include verses to look up)

A mother and her sons

Share: Describe a power struggle you've had with your children or your parents.

Prayer: Seek God together on what it looks like for you to love your children or your parents fearlessly.

Loving Fearlessly

Constant contact

Share: Describe your 21st Century connectivity. Are there ways you try to stay connected with people as a substitute for your connection with God?

Prayer: Spend time abiding with Jesus and listening to him.

More than enough

Share: Describe a personal struggle with being enough/having enough.

Prayer: Share with each other in prayer the riches and goodness of God. (Ephesians 1:3-14; 2 Peter 1:3-4)

Walking the walk

Share: Where are you currently going? Who are you leading or following?

Prayer: Take time individually naming the people or things that have their hooks in you. Then come to the waters of repentance together, letting the Spirit wash over you and the fire of forgiveness burn away all fears of punishment.

Breaking the silence

Share: Who have you forgiven and who are you holding out on?

Prayer: Practice four-way forgiveness together.

Becoming bread

Share: In what areas of your life is it hard to believe God for miracles?

Prayer: Pray together to be broken and multiplied by faith.

About the Author

Rachael Sanowski grew up on Lake St. Clair in Harrison Township, Michigan. She studied English and German at the University of Michigan. She also studied abroad at the Albert-Ludwigs-Universität in Freiburg, Germany, where she fell in love with a German and eventually married him. After two lovely years in Freiburg-Opfingen, she and Christoph headed to Detroit, Michigan around the time of the 2000 census, when African Americans comprised 85% of the city population and whites comprised 70% of the surrounding suburban population. Early in the new millennium, they bought a house in southwest Detroit, where they still reside with their three children. They attend Mosaic Midtown Church.

The Detroit streets have been Rachael's beat for over 15 years. She taught three years of high school English and German and then returned to school to earn her Master of Education in Counseling at Wayne State University. She has worked as a licensed counselor at Covenant Community Care Clinic since 2008. She loves journeying with people in grief and worship and welcoming people into safe and revolutionary spaces.

Detroit is changing so quickly. Buildings are either being demolished or refurbished. Investors in Portugal are buying up foreclosed properties. The Gordie Howe Bridge is taking out part of Rachael's street. Her son, Gabe, says their neighborhood is unwillingly becoming a road to somewhere else. New restaurants and new faces are everywhere. Segregation is moving *into* the city. Christoph and Rachael recently tried to go out to eat on a Saturday night without a reservation. They found a new place on Michigan Avenue, down the street from the New Life Rescue Mission. They went through a 16-foot fence and entered a neon lighted dining space filled with white staff and patrons and were told it would be about a 2-hour wait before they could be seated.

Whatever the future holds for her (and Detroit), Rachael wants to keep living and loving fearlessly, as her Good Shepherd leads and loves the fear right out of her.

www.ingramcontent.com/pod-product-compliance
Ingram Content Group UK Ltd.
Pitfield, Milton Keynes, MK11 3LW, UK
UKHW062313290726
14090UKWH00018B/1046

9 781532 367175